Unapologetically Anxious Me
Confessions, Stories and Musings of a Haitian American Girl

Josette 'Jo' Ciceron

Dedication

This book is dedicated to my always shining Rina, my brilliant Lex, and the man who has watched me go through it all and has gotten down in the trenches with me. If not for him, I may have never gained the courage to write these words—my Lanau. You all will never fully understand what an anchor you are in my life. Thank you for helping me truly live for love alone…

Table of Contents

Dedication	3
Introduction	7
Chapter 1 ~ The Night That Changed Everything	11
Chapter 2 ~ Lekol, Legliz, Lakay (School, Church, Home)	20
Chapter 3 ~ Wherefore Art	34
Thou Love	34
Chapter 4 ~ The Start of Something New	42
Chapter 5 ~ I Came Out of the Womb Winding My Hips!	52
Chapter 6 ~Daddy's Girl	64
Chapter 7 ~ Once Upon These Days	73
Chapter 8 ~ Starting Us Over	85
Chapter 9 ~ She Never Said a Word	102
Chapter 10 ~ My Dark Passenger	110
Chapter 11 ~ Family Matters	127
Chapter 12 ~ Simply Complicated	142
Chapter 13 ~ Just Call Me Boo Radley	162
Chapter 14 ~ Unfinished Story	182
About the Author	192
Special Thanks	194

Introduction

I have a confession to make. Though I have a podcast entitled, Unapologetically Anxious Me and now this book, the real me is very much apologetic. Some would believe it is a side-effect of the "Minnesota Nice" syndrome I've picked up since living here over the past five years, but I know that's not true. I've been saying, "I'm sorry" in one form or another ever since I could speak.

I apologize for virtually everything. No, really, I do—passing someone too closely at the store, getting in someone's way, for others' pain and situations, for living, for breathing—for existing. Just the other day I was on a call with a friend as she was heading to go to work. We remained on FaceTime for a little while as she drove and she suddenly said, "Shoot, I forgot my charger!" And without hesitation, I told her I was sorry, and she asked me, "Why are you apologizing to me? You had nothing to do with my forgetting!"

Though we both laughed it off as "Jo just doing Jo things," it made me recall the moment I first realized this had become a pretty bad problem. In the summer of 2019 my friend and colleague, Pree, and I, along with a local organization called the Inclusion Network (IN), came together in solidarity to create a talk show that would bring everyday members of our small community to the table to have frank, open, and honest conversations about social issues that affect us all.

In support of me and my experiences in Alexandria, Minnesota, they not only encouraged me, they gave me space to create my own seat at the table. Together, we brought my dream to life by creating the "Voices Talk Show."

At the start of filming every episode, I met with my panelists on set just before filming. Towards the end of our first season, I filmed an episode about mental health in our farming communities. I briefed everyone on what to expect and collected media consent forms—all while we were being mic'd up and placed in the spaces around the table that were best suited for our camera team's liking.

As the panelists settled into their seats, I rambled on about what everyone should be aware of during filming. One of the panelists, who was also the only other woman at the table that day, abruptly interrupted me and asked, "Do you know I've heard you apologize over 10 times and I've only known you for about 15 minutes?!" Everyone around the table fell quiet.

I wanted to crumble into my seat and disappear. I was embarrassed. Although I kinda always knew that I did this, I didn't know people actually took notice. She continued and said, "I don't mean to call you out. I just think you're too amazing a woman to feel the need to apologize for things men are never expected to apologize for." And she was completely right. I couldn't help but thank her for putting this right in front of me to face and overcome.

Welp, your girl is not quite there yet! Being unapologetic for me is a skill and strength I still long to conquer. I am blessed to work with one of the best hired friends a girl can ask for! Therapy was and still is the best move I ever made for myself. It wasn't until I developed that third eye that I realized just how much my mental health has affected my life and the choices I've made for myself. Though I'm no expert or doctor, I am an expert on my own life and can only speak to my own personal experiences.

Writing a book has been on my mind ever since I was a child. As an adult over the years, I started writing and then would stop—convincing myself it just wasn't the right time. In fact, I could vividly remember writing a "When I grow up I'm going to be…" essay where I proclaimed myself to be an "author" honing her craft. The day my second-grade teacher, Ms. Lake introduced me to the art of storytelling through writing—I was hooked. To this day, I still have a large plastic storage container filled with composition notebooks of my writing through the ages (first grade to beyond senior year in high school).

I've always adored the art of storytelling. Whether I was writing it, consuming it, or listening to it—my relationship with the written word is the one relationship I can always depend on, and it will always be part of me. In many ways, writing raised me. Writing educated me. Writing healed me. This book is the ultimate and most difficult form of therapy I've experienced since I was diagnosed with anxiety, depression, and PTSD in 2016.

Throughout the pages of this book, I hope you find comfort, insight, reality, and a true vision of my heart. I hope it makes you smile. I hope it makes you laugh—you may even cry a little—sorry in advance (See? Told you it's a problem)! You can also assume any conversation happening between me and my parents or Haitian adults are being translated from Creole to English. Above all—I hope to truly reach you wherever you may find yourself right now.

In the words of actress and Black mental health advocate, Taraji P. Henson from her "Peace of Mind" talk show on Facebook Watch: "We gon' heal DAMN IT!"

TRIGGER WARNING:

My story is written from a place of truth and my longing to speak my truth. There are words and stories that may trigger negative emotions. Please be aware of this before you continue. Names and identities have been altered of some of the characters to protect their privacy.

Chapter 1 ~ The Night That Changed Everything

"Nothing is absolute. Everything changes, everything moves, everything revolves, everything flies and goes away."

~Frida Khalo

Lanau and I knelt on the wooden floor in the middle of the hallway of my childhood home. My mom and dad stood over us, arms extended in the air in worship-form as they prayed over us. Eyes closed tightly, both passionately had separate conversations with God as Lanau and I occasionally exchanged unsure glances with each other.

I can honestly say I felt relief walking into my parents' house that evening…I was 27 years old, married for just under two years and had a wonderful one-year-old son, Lenoxx. Our foray into married life collided with the devastating and dwindling Florida job economy. For over six months we both intensely and earnestly looked for work, hemorrhaging funds and quickly burning through the minuscule amount of money we'd managed to save from years of intense work.

It was summertime in 2015 and I'd just been laid off from my job as a college admissions advisor, and Lanau's job, which was at a marketing company, carried out their round of lay-offs only two months after mine.

Now, here we were in the middle of my parents' home doing what we'd sworn we would never do, not after managing to escape the lockdown, sheltered, too-small town, suffocating Haitian community life that was living at home in "Fort Misery" (better known as Fort Myers, Florida). Lanau and I had just spent the last two weeks of our lives gradually losing everything we'd worked for. We were evicted from our apartment, had our car repossessed, and got to the point where we could hardly afford food for ourselves.

Lanau and I both listened to my parents, who were practically screaming as they said their prayers. At first, I wasn't at all thrown off by the ritual simply because this was life for me growing up with my insanely strict, religious, controlling, and hella old-school Haitian parents' home.

My mom and dad are devout Baptist Christians who have quite literally devoted their lives to their faith. My father's Christian work commenced as a deacon at our fairly large Haitian church. By the time I started my college years, he had gone back to school to complete his ministry studies and became a pastor—a role he'd been performing at our home church unofficially for most of my life.

My mother is a simple Caribbean housewife who takes A LOT of pride in the life she's built with my father and uses faith as her guiding post in everything she does in life—and I mean everything. Since she was super talented in seamstress work, I always imagined she'd eventually make a career out of it or start a business, especially considering how many favors she did for friends and family over the years—by offering up her services to tailor people's clothing for a very good price, if at any cost at all.

Up until I was in the sixth grade, she made a majority of my school ensembles—much to my dismay. While she was talented at making clothing, I certainly didn't share her affinity for prairie-style dresses with tiers and layers, lots of lace trimming with matching hair ribbons—and bonnets. Yeah—you read that correctly—bonnets. The whimsical or downright tacky fabric patterns of polka dots, or better yet, polka-dotted hearts (insert face palm emoji!). To add insult to injury, there was always an array of weird giant buttons attached to these ensembles which didn't make me the "it" fashion girl amongst my peers.

I hated them! She thought I was an ungrateful spoiled brat who didn't appreciate the hard work she put into making my clothing. In her eyes, she was too good to dress her daughters in cheaply made clothing with characters on them as she'd witnessed from other parents in the states. Little did she know I would have gladly worn the 101 Dalmatians shorts with the matching t-shirt from Kmart for $7.00—over the poofy dress that not only required a slip dress and ruffle underwear, but also required the assistance of a crinoline to truly help it stand out in all of its glory.

Extremely proper, my mom was obsessed with keeping a clean house, a pristine, always together, and tailored physical appearance, and being a "good" Christian. She legit cannot go two sentences without bringing God, church, or Christianity into it—which made it pretty much impossible to have just a normal conversation with my mother. A stern, no-nonsense, serious, and matter-of-fact lady, she believes a woman's role in life is to serve God, her husband and raise children to someday become hard-working Christian members of society.

As I knelt on the floor, I suddenly realized my poor husband was not used to the intensity of this life that I knew all too well. Life at home meant I was practically tunneling my way out of my room with a spoon as a child to escape the incessant militant-like hold religion had on me and my parents' way of life.

So here we are and I'm thinking, "Here it is. That love and support I always wanted from them!" ...And then I began listening closer to their prayers. They each were thanking God for bringing me and Lenoxx "home to them during this difficult time in my life." They shouted about how they wished for God to rid me of my "burdens" and to finally "save me" from this life I'd apparently been "suffering" from.

By this point Lanau and I were staring straight at one another, both of us knowing something was not right. Amidst all their shouting and dramatic gesticulations in this apparent negotiation with God—not a single word was ever uttered or even acknowledged about Lanau as a part of my family.

Before I could fully grasp what was going on, they asked the two of us to rise to our feet as my mom said to me, "Come into the bedroom so your father and I can talk to you." Then, as if they'd been rehearsing this moment prior to our arrival, my dad jumped in suddenly, addressing Lanau. "Lanau, go home to your mother's house. We'll take care of Josette from here."

Baffled, Lanau and I continued to look at each other in complete disbelief over what was being said to us. My mother and father basically were making the decision for us to separate maritally! Lanau's look of confusion immediately morphed into hurt, betrayal, and then anger. Something in me—in that moment—snapped.

Pissed and just so hurt, I lost it on my parents in a way I've never done in my life! I couldn't believe that they'd just manipulated me into believing they were actually going to take us into the spare loft they'd built onto the house after I moved out to go to college in Tampa.

I felt crushed. I trusted them in a way I'd always known I couldn't. But for the first time in my adult life, I took their word at face value and believed they genuinely wanted to give my family the support we desperately needed to stabilize our lives and get back on our feet. We could not have been more wrong.

My parents never had any intention to help me get my life back together—they sought this opportunity to finally be rid of the daughter's husband they didn't like—and never would.

Completely enraged with my parents' words and actions, we yelled and shouted as I paced throughout the house, eventually ending up in the living room with my parents in tow. I was so overwhelmed by emotion that I was almost inaudible. I couldn't watch Lanau go through this any longer and demanded he go outside and wait for me.

Confused at the commotion around him, Lenoxx ran up to me with his arms spread out to be picked up. His eyes welled up with tears and the fear in them was gut-wrenching. I scooped him up, panting hard and unsure of what to do next. He was crying at this point, and I could not help but join him.

"Look at yourself Josette—you can't take care of your

child," my dad said, looking at me with complete pity. I felt my insides crumbling. The words pierced through me like a knife. From the corner of my eye, I saw my mother approaching me, reaching to take Lenoxx out of my arms. Maybe my maternal instincts were kicking in, but suddenly that hold, that fear, that control they had over me was broken in an instant and I was seeing them in their purest form.

I was heartbroken. All the memories of being isolated, controlled, manipulated, and made to feel less than inferior as a child came crashing down on me. At that moment—I knew I had nothing left to be afraid of. I glared at my mother with a defiance I know neither of us had ever witnessed from me and told them both to back off. This time—I was going to say my piece and they were going to listen.

Flipping from Creole to English, I spoke firmly. "It's one thing to manipulate me into coming here...with my family, thinking you guys could actually be supporting me! I was so stupid to believe that, after years of doing the complete opposite and feeling like nothing I ever did was good enough for you—NOW you're trying to take my son—my family, away from me?! What did I ever do to you guys to deserve that?!"

I was shaking at this point, and I could feel Lenoxx's little body gripping onto me out of fear. My father tried to interrupt, but I held firm with my arm extended out in front of me, cut him off, and continued speaking. "NO daddy. Not this time. I will NOT take this from you anymore! You told me to be open and to let you in! You told me to give you guys the chance to help me. So, I did. And it killed me! I knew what admitting failure meant in this family. I knew what being vulnerable earned you and still I willed myself to tell you that I had, in fact, failed. That I had lost my job.

That we were struggling and that we needed a moment to catch our breaths."

Every so often my mother piped in with her usual smart remarks, claiming how I don't ever listen to anyone and that I am just so hard to talk to…a notion I have to admit literally stopped me dead in the middle of my rant to laugh at the pure ridiculousness of the comment itself, especially coming from them.

My mother has never been known to be the kind of person you could come to and speak about your feelings or open up about your innermost, personal thoughts. After a lifetime of sticking my toe in the fire—I finally learned that the shit burns and to just stay away.

I don't know exactly what they heard or took in from me that evening, but one thing should have manifested itself loud and clear: the little girl, the one they had complete mental and emotional control over—no longer existed. I was a mother, and I knew I was a damn good one. I knew I had done nothing to deserve this type of treatment. I also knew my relationship with my mother and father was forever altered and possibly past the point of repair.

They both fell back and seemed unsure of what to do next, exchanging looks of disbelief and aggravation. We'd been arguing for well over an hour and getting nowhere. After a moment of silence, my dad started up again, trying to explain why leaving my husband was the best move and to at least try a separation for a while to see how I felt. Not even justifying any of it with a response, I held on tightly to Lenoxx and walked out of the house without saying a word. They both called after me, saying whatever they could to make me submit to them.

My father followed me outside, still pleading with me to listen to their reasoning. Almost Shakespearean in irony, rain began to fall and was gradually getting heavier as I made my way out to the car, the lights cutting through the darkness. After seeing the emotional wreckage that covered my face, Lanau got out from the driver's side to meet me. As I passed off our trembling son to Lanau to get strapped into the car seat, I thought about how foolish I'd been to believe these people ever wanted to truly support me.

Before pulling out, my father ran up to the driver's side of the car and shouted sneeringly to Lanau, "You know you're going to kill my daughter?! You're making her suffer! Let me take care of her and you go back to your mom!" The words seared my mind and heart as we drove away knowing I could do nothing but watch Lanau's clear and honest hurt.

Astounded by what we'd both experienced, I told Lanau to drive to his mother's house so I could collect myself. I couldn't believe I had not seen it coming. Walking into the familiar home, I was immediately shifted back into an emotional whirlwind as Lanau's mother greeted us with shock and bewilderment as she told us my father had just called her screaming and cursing her out.

He was telling her how he believed her son was ruining my life and that it was her fault. Along with a myriad of insults, he demanded she make her son "release" me back to him so he could have the opportunity to "fix me up" again. As I write these words, I wish so badly that my words weren't literal or complete truth; one thing you should know about me and my life—it certainly needs no embellishment.

This is honestly just who my parents were. It had been

nearly eight years since I'd left their home in January of 2008. Living on my own in Tampa, I had allowed myself to slip into a false sense of security that my parents not only saw me as an individual who could be trusted to make her own sound decisions—I believed they wanted me to be happy on my own terms and respected where I was in my life.

What happened that night changed the entire trajectory of my life. That night the two people who were supposed to love me unconditionally, who gave me my life's blood, had no respect for who I really was. None of the physical, mental, sexual, or even emotional abuse demons of my past could surpass the level of pain that one night alone has inscribed on my heart and in my psyche.

I do think it's important to note how much I love my parents. I am evolved enough to understand that they do love me, in their own unique ways. A lot of what I experienced in my life was not at their hands, but it certainly occurred as a result of who they are and who they were portrayed to me growing up.

Within 24 hours of that fateful night, Lanau and I had no choice but to make some hard decisions. Lanau's brother, John, and his wife Michelle (at the time) offered to fly us to Minnesota so we could stay with them for about six months or so, until we got back on our feet. Many may not understand the extremity of the path we took, but we now know it was the best path for us at the time. Small-town Minnesota was never part of our plan, but it's essentially where our evolution truly began.

Chapter 2 ~ Lekol, Legliz, Lakay (School, Church, Home)

"I am my own muse. I am the subject I know best. The subject I want to know better."

~Frida Khalo

Like most Caribbean and African Continental parents, Haitians were known to be incredibly strict with their children who were growing up in the states. I'd be watching a 90s sitcom and my mom would walk into the room just as the actor playing the hormonal, angry teenager role would start screaming and talking back to their parents, saying something along the lines of, "Ugh, you're ruining my life!" This would usually be followed by the slamming of a bedroom door. My mom would chuckle and threaten sarcastically, "Try me one good time with that White people shit and watch what happens…" This was her version of the common saying, "I brought you into this world and I will take you out!" saying.

"Lekol (school), Legliz (church), and Lakay (home) was practically a moniker for Haitian parenting when I was growing up. While some Haitian parents raising children in the states were laxer and more Americanized than others, that certainly wasn't the case for most of us. If I had to fit my parents into a spectrum of sorts, they would be tipping off the more extreme side. In our house, those were the only parent-approved places to go to spend any length of time.

To their dismay, my parents just so happen to be blessed with a child (ME!) who wanted to go everywhere and anywhere! With parents working all the time I was positive the main cause of death before age 15 was going to be boredom! I loved making friends and spending time with them. If they were American, I was never allowed to go to their houses though, they were allowed to come to mine—and only after my dad would awkwardly, embarrassingly, and intensely interrogate them about who they were as people, and whether they believed in God. The amount of deep sighing and face-palming I did growing up—I could've been the actual face of that emoji.

The interrogation was usually the part I'd hold my breath and wait for the other parent to tell him to go screw himself. I was always shocked when they agreed to let their kid spend the night at the strange man's house. Nonetheless, I was always excited to feel like a normal kid who got to hang out with friends outside of a classroom.

Even though it was a rare occurrence, I liked bringing my friends into my world and tried my hardest to appear "normal." I remember one first-grade friend, Maisey, who was the first white girl to sleepover at our house. Though I was worried she'd be bored because I didn't own any cool toys or games—what she cared most about was how different we lived, and she loved it. She thought my dad was funny, our food was good, and in general, she loved the life that I couldn't wait to grow up and be free of.

RANDOM RANT: As a kid I was convinced my parents were committed to my eternal boredom. No, really. There was an excuse for any reason why I could not or would not do or have anything. Of course, we weren't flush with cash but we were doing okay. When I'd ask for toys or games I was usually met with annoyance or anger as to how I could possibly ask such an absurd question. I'd be reminded how hard they have to work for everything. How they didn't even have the audacity to ask for such things when they were my age and so on and so forth. Just suggesting we do something fun as a family like go to the beach or the park was an issue. They'd tell me I was spoiled or they'd remind me of all the many dangers of being in those places—from abduction to drowning, I very quickly learned it's better to not ask at all.

The following Sunday morning, we took her to church with us and she was even more excited about that. When Maisey saw my mom pull-out my super ruffly, tiered, satin, and lace-trimmed pink dress. She screeched with delight and marveled at the collection of what she called, "princess dresses" in my closet—ALL of which I detested.

Smack dab in a predominantly White town in Fort Myers, Florida, my family was part of a rather large, close-knit Haitian community. This meant everyone knew your parents and took that whole "it takes a village" mindset literally. If you were daring enough to misbehave in the presence of any Haitian adult in the early afternoon, you could guarantee your parents would have heard all about it from Ser 'So and So' ("Sister So and So") before the streetlights even came on and you stepped inside the house. You can certainly expect a backhanded slap is forthcoming.

As I got closer to my preteen years, and after being made fun of or sometimes excluded from groups in elementary school, I found my core group of friends and they were all Haitian American like me. Mynoucka, Gertrude, and Faye were my best friends growing up and until this day we remain friends who love each other. Though life has taken us all to different places, I'm still grateful for the first group of people who made me feel like I had real people in my life to depend on. In many ways they too, took part in raising me into the woman I am today.

We all lived similar lives, our parents socialized together and were part of the same circles and church. They understood my strict home life—though I think we could all agree then and even more now—that my parents were a special brand of Haitian parenting that would even leave my Haitian friends' parents feeling a bit for me.

Their parents were stringent, but they still came from families that knew each other and spent real time together outside of a church service. I was jealous of the real conversations they could have with their moms as they got older without being verbally obliterated for trying to ask questions or talk about their feelings.

All I ever wanted was to be part of a real family and have real friends to confide in. And while I did, for the most part, I knew there were facets of my life I just could never share with my friends.

My family was well-known in Fort Misery, but after getting heavily into the church they became more withdrawn, less friendly, and very secretive. Being the chatty one of the bunch, I was always being warned to not speak on this or never repeat that. They'd poke fun at me for being a blabbermouth and would get very angry when I slipped up in front of their friends.

My parents' expectations of my two sisters and I were sky-high and until we were out of their house, paying our own bills, what we thought, felt, or wanted was irrelevant. On almost a weekly basis my dad would tell me how blessed we were to live in a country where we got to go to school for free as a child. Schooling in Haiti in the 50s and 60s was not free for anyone to attend.

Unless you were part of a wealthy family, which still makes up less than two percent of the country's upper class today you likely didn't make it through high school or further because your family and parents couldn't afford it. This would be why neither of my parents ever got very far in high school—if they made it to that grade level at all.

There is nothing an old school Haitian parent enjoys more than a good ole comparison. Such comparisons happened to me and my sisters at several points throughout our lives. "Why can't you be more like Josette?" they'd say to Carline when we were little because I took an interest in church, reading the Bible in Creole, and singing and dancing. As I became an adult it flipped and I spent the better part of my twenties being bombarded with comparisons to Carline's educational choices, her romantic choices, and career choices.

While my parents believed these judgments and comparisons were keeping us sharp and on our toes. In actuality, they kept us separated as our resentment over the years grew stronger for one another and we became less and less inclined to trust each other let alone maintain a friendship.

This would probably be why I later kept so much from my family in fear of exposing my failures. Even then I knew admitting defeat didn't come with a "that's okay" or "you'll figure it out next time." It came in the form of harsh and relentless criticisms that would quickly take me down a few notches in my confidence every time I handed them the ammunition.

My parents are first-generation immigrants who migrated from Haiti in the early 80s. Now and then it hits me that my parents were just around their mid-20s when they moved their little family to the states—taking a leap of faith in starting over in a new country with no family or financial support. I was born in Asbury Park, NJ in the fall of 1987 with an unexpected pregnancy. My father was elated—my mother was not so much.

Not being citizens of this country back then left them with very few options for employment, so they typically picked up jobs that were extremely labor-intensive working in factories, restaurants, hotels, industrial laundry, and healthcare facilities which offered housekeeping and janitorial positions. For most of my life, my parents held down two jobs or more determined to create a life of stability for their children.

Looking back now and being a parent myself, I can see why they made certain decisions and the sacrifices they made to take care of us. Being their only American-born child, they along with the rest of my family never missed an opportunity to remind me how blessed and fortunate I was. I can still remember my sister before me, Carline, and our oldest sister, Asmite, studying together to take their US citizenship exams.

Sometime soon after them, my father also became a US citizen. I remember this clearly because while I was learning about the president and state capitals—so was my dad in preparation for his exam. Having worked so hard to make it to the states, I loved seeing the pride and pure joy of accomplishing his lifelong dream of being an American.

Much like me, my dad loved to learn. Outside the Bible, he would pour over all kinds of literature, history, and anything he believed elevated his understanding of the world around him. My favorite moments with him as a child was just hearing about the random facts he'd absorbed through the pages of a book. His love for reading only ignited my thirst for the written word.

As a kid I'd watch shows like *Full House*, *Sabrina the Teenage Witch*, and *Boy Meets World* and knew my family's home differed greatly from my White American peers and classmates. Just bringing lunch to school as a kid made me stand out which was the last thing I needed.

Believing that all things American cuisine were awful for you, my dad packed my lunch into an elaborate and ornate Haitian version of a Tupperware bowl. The most typical meal was diri blan, sos pwa noir, avec sos poule (white rice, black bean sauce with stewed chicken)—all mixed up like our parents typically do for us when we're younger. And off he sent me with my Beauty & the Beast lunchbox.

Of course, when you're in second grade the "Ewww! What is that?!" are awfully hard to avoid when you're surrounded by American kids and are usually the only person of color in class. PLUS—do you know what black beans smell like when they've been in a sealed container since the early morning?! Who knows! But knowing my dad he probably assumed they provided second graders access to a microwave in the school cafeteria—and that was definitely not the case. Naturally, any complaints I made at the time would be rebutted with accusations of being ungrateful for parents who went out of their way to make organic home-cooked meals that they were convinced were far healthier than the processed American foods they have seen kids eating on TV.

My childhood in comparison to most first-generation Haitian people's children was relatively normal. Our parents were working low-income jobs, and often multiple at a time. The only time our family got together to do anything, was for prayer, eating out, or them telling us all about the random story of growing up in Haiti that was meant to either scare the shit out of us or teach us some lesson that would prevent us from even thinking about it.

Haitian parents were pros at preventative parenting which always came with a shit ton of "don't do this" and "never do that's." If someone's teen daughter got pregnant from our church or even within the Haitian community, that would be every parent's go-to life-lesson of the week. We'd all heard whisperings and rumors about said pregnant individual's parents sending her to Haiti to avoid the looks of shame and ridicule that was sure to come to her parents for allowing something like that to happen.

In the 90s all Haitian parents seemed to be on this American-kids-are-a-bad-influence kick which made it so you really couldn't have much of a social life outside of our community unless you were willing to deal with the consequences—whoopings. Today, you'll likely hear many Haitian and even Caribbean adults joke about their regular whoopings growing up whenever you were in trouble.

One of the first things you'd hear as you walk into the house would be, "Al fout mete-ou a-jenou!" which the literal translation for that would be "Go get on your fucking knees!" This was the bat signal letting you and everyone else around you know that some real shit was about to go down. And as you remained knelt down you could sit there and panic about the pain you knew was sure to come.

Some parents used a belt while others used a switch—if they were angry enough their weapon of choice would be whatever happens to be lying around. The severity of the lashing would be based on the severity of what you may or may not have done. As kids growing up in America, we were well-aware that this was considered child abuse and were all well-trained to never say a word.

Every now and then, we heard a story about a kid telling a schoolteacher the truth behind their scars and bruises. This always led to the child being removed from the home and in most cases if their parents were immigrants they were deported back to Haiti. That kid then ended up in the American foster system which most of us would agree was a far worse fate than a sound lashing.

My parents were no different though they each dealt their whoopings out much differently. My dad was the level-headed parent who you'd have to have really done something big for him to feel the need to punish you. Unlike my mom, he usually would tell you why this is happening and would justify his actions with a biblical reference.

Looking back now, I knew it was all bullshit, but I knew

who I was and I knew inside the walls of our home they held all the power. No one wanted to see their families destroyed by the system in a country that didn't value people of color—especially immigrants.

My mom was the reactor. She was quick to anger and quicker to snap. Her levels of anger rarely had much to do with something we had done wrong but more so her overall annoyance with being a mom and working a 40-hour-a-week housekeeping job that only paid minimum wage. She was always crabby and you felt the energy shift in the air as soon as she got home.

No one wanted to piss her off because not only are you liable to be back-handed at any given moment—she'd also lecture you for literally hours. There were arguments she had with my oldest sister, Asmite who was a teenager at the time, that would start at six in the evening and would go well into mid-morning the next day. She repeated these cycles with Carline and then me.

My dad was as loving as he was for the most part—the older my sisters got, the more short-tempered he became, and the beatings became much harsher. There was one evening when my parents left me home alone with my two older sisters who were around 13 and 17–years old at the time. They weren't going to be back until after midnight and so my sisters saw this as their opportunity to attend a teen house party one of Asmite's friends was having.

They left me home alone and told me they'd be back soon. They even ordered my favorite food at the time, which was a pepperoni pizza from Papa John's. I was solid for the night and was pretty excited to be home by myself for the first time. I must've been eight or nine when this took place.

It was well past midnight and my parents called on their way home per the norm. Half asleep, I picked up the phone and they immediately asked me why I wasn't asleep yet. I panicked a little when I realized Asmite and Carline weren't home yet. "Where's your sisters?" My dad asked.

Too flustered to lie to my dad who had that I-know-something-isn't-right sound in his voice, I searched my mind for what to say next. Yelling at me through the phone he shouted, "Josette?! Where are Asmite and Carline?!"

Already in tears and whimpering, afraid of what was coming, all I could manage was to quietly say, "I don't know…." Like a sped-up scene in a cartoon, my dad hung up abruptly and before I knew it, he was storming through the door with my mom following close behind, already talking up a storm.

They both yelled at me, demanding I tell them where my sisters went. I knew somewhat but didn't know details about where they were for sure. Done with attempting answers out of me, dad stormed out of the house, got back into the car, and pulled out the driveway—clearly on a mission to find my sisters no matter what.

I don't know how he figured out where they were—but after what felt like an eternity, the front door swung open suddenly as my sister ran swiftly to Asmite's room. I was in my bedroom across the hall from them. She and Carline scurried through the living room so fast by the time my dad had made it into the hallway—their room door was locked firmly between them.

I watched anxiously from the threshold across the hall, bewildered by what was taking place. Sure, we'd gotten into our fair share of trouble and have had whoopings for as long as I could remember. But this time was different. I don't think I'd ever seen my father so angry as he banged on the bedroom door to be let in.

You'd think my mom would be trying to keep him calm and tell him not to lose his temper. Instead, she was talking up a storm in the background about where my sisters were and who they were with. She said every horrible thing you could possibly say about a daughter as my dad grew angrier and angrier.

Not sure if it was just standing in a corner nearby but with one single blow—my dad rammed a broomstick directly into the bedroom creating a small hole—breaking the broom in the process. He was yelling belligerently and behaving in a way I'd never seen before. In the background, I screamed and begged for him to stop.

My mother whipped around to look at me with cold eyes—threatening me to shut my mouth if I didn't want to be next. Ever the empath, I began crying hysterically in the background after a second blow caused the bedroom door to fling open. I watched in horror as my father dragged Carline's body from under the bed. She let out a wail, I'd never heard in my life, and all I could do was sob as my father beat her first with his belt and then with a piece of 2x4 wooden plank that had been holding the bed up, he'd just pulled her from.

Every detail of that night remains carved into my memory like an open wound that remains pulsating with pain. With it comes all the memories of these "whoopings" as we so casually come to discuss them today as fleeting musings from our past. I can only imagine how many of them still bear the inner bruises that were left behind from such intense and abusive means of yielding obedient children.

My dad would tell me how it's his duty as a parent to teach me how to be obedient so I could be a proper woman one day which always baited the question "for whom?"—though I'd never have been foolish enough to ask that out loud.

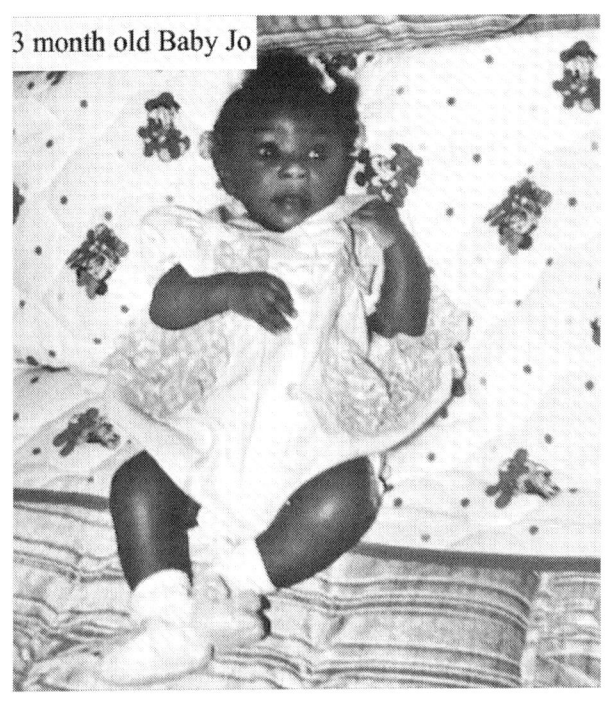
3 month old Baby Jo

Chapter 3 ~ Wherefore Art Thou Love

"I am that clumsy human, always loving, loving, loving. And loving. And never leaving."

~Frida Khalo

For as long as I could remember I'd been dreaming of a perfect love. The kind of love that knows no boundaries, goes beyond human limitations and fuses two souls in a way that will never be understood by those who live outside of it. As a kid who grew up in a home limited with entertainment, toys, and access to cable TV, I very quickly learned that my parents couldn't care less so long as it looked like I was doing something productive and staying out of their hair.

My parents were rarely home due to balancing multiple jobs to maintain a life in America. Such a privilege comes at a much higher rate of attainability for many immigrants, as well as many Brown and Black Americans who suffer a similar fate due to their lack of access. My parents were rarely home and worked twice as hard as most people did just to get by and provide the basics for their children.

Reading was my escape. Through the pages of my books, I could travel far and wide to just about anywhere my mind could imagine up. The more I read, the more I realized that my mind could reach just about every corner of the Earth in just a few eloquently sewn-together words. I found reading to be magical and the first sense of power and euphoria I'd ever had the pleasure of experiencing.

Through literature, I was able to peek into the equally conflicted minds of adults which was captivating as a lonely child who was not given much space to be myself—free of criticisms and ridicule.

Above all else—I learned early on that I truly loved love. I saw love in different aspects of my upbringing. For instance, I knew my father was madly in love with my mother. I saw it in the way he made it a habit to put a smile on her face even if it was just Wednesday. I could always tell how much he enjoyed taking care of her and putting her first. Something that even 37 years of marriage later he has yet to falter from.

Whether it was Christmas, Valentine's Day, or a birthday—he always had a plan to make her feel special. I admired his commitment to her and as a little girl always excited to be let in on his secret plan or better yet tag along on a trip to a jewelry store for just the right gift that would make her smile. I swore I'd marry a man who did the same for me.

My father was the first type of love I'd ever experienced. Even as a child who barely knew herself or anything of the world she lived in, I knew whatever I did in life as long as I had true love surrounding me, I'd always be happy.

I wasn't always sure if my mom enjoyed this attention or if she shared the same intense love for my father as—from my perspective as a kid, at least, it seemed rather tame in comparison to my dad's frequent thoughtful gestures.

When my dad gave her a gift that was all wrapped up, she never liked opening the gifts right away or in front of us. I remember a few times she got annoyed with us kids along with my dad for trying to make her open something that was "given to just her." I never quite understood it and felt sad for my dad knowing he was excited to give her these gifts—especially when my sisters and I were involved in the picking process.

When it came to doing the same for my father, she'd frequently scoff at the idea of making plans or buying a gift on daddy's birthday or Father's Day. She usually laughed dismissively at the mere request from me to do so—often replying with a sarcastic remark like, "With what money?" Or one of her favorite go-to sayings was, "Do you know how many bills we have piling up to worry about paying for?!" This was swiftly followed by a long-winded lecture about how spoiled or ungrateful we were as children for even wanting gifts for ourselves for Christmas. And that because of us she couldn't experience the finer things in life—as if she seriously believed we had a say so in our conception.

While I didn't understand her perspective fully on the finances as a kid, I just wondered why my dad always made something happen—even during the years where he just couldn't swing a nicer gift financially. He'd make her dinner or take her out to eat. During good times he'd whisk her off to a nice hotel for a weekend to get her out of the house which stressed her out to maintain while being a working mother of three. I knew while we lived okay for an immigrant family—however, we were not by any means wealthy. Though many of my parents' friends and families in Haiti believed they were living the good life.

I met Lanau when I was about seven or eight years old. Our

mothers were working as housekeepers together in an industrial laundry facility and had somehow connected in the mid-90s over their love of yard sales.

Yard sales in our Haitian community were a favorite weekend pastime because most of our parents were devoted to taking care of their families back on the island. So, hunting for good bargains meant one more opportunity to send things home to help provide for their poverty-ridden relatives and neighbors. (This is a tradition upheld by many immigrants who come to the United States in search of a better life.) To be the first to make it out of the grips of perpetual poverty in Haiti comes with certain obligations.

My parents, like most of our fellow Haitian friends and neighbors, had this sense of duty because they had the privilege to live in a developed country where an income, purpose, and even access were a normal part of life. I can still remember the profound awakening I had when I visited Haiti for the first time at the age of seven. Only then did I realize what a privilege it was to wake up, turn on a faucet and get fresh running water to brush my teeth with or to prepare a hot cup of automatically made coffee.

Asmite and Carline were out and about minding their teenaged business as I was left inside the house to just exist until someone came home again. As his mother nudged him into our dining room, it was obvious Lanau did not want to be there. With what I presume was a Game Boy in his hands, he huffed, puffed, and groaned as his mother told him to just deal until she returned and that she'd be back before he knew it.

My oldest sister was left "in charge" which meant as soon

as the place was cleared of adults, she'd be off doing her own thing, leaving me to fend for myself. As a courtesy to the new kid in the room, she asked Lanau, who couldn't have been more than nine-years-old at the time, whether he was hungry or needed anything. With a single annoyed groan, he declined and focused on his game.

For hours we sat in the same room as he ignored me. At one point I tried to tell him about some cool books I had in my room but he gave me that "you're-just-a-dumb-kid" look and I never broke the too-cool-for-school, grumpy kid's concentration again.

His mom came back to claim him as promised a few painfully long hours later and we would not see or hear of each other again for at least another eight years when we ended up attending the same high school.

Lanau and I graduated from the same high school. He was two grades ahead of me (class of 2004) and we honestly never seen each other in a romantic way. In fact, for the last two years of his high school career, we were just not friends. We shared my best friend, Mynoucka, whom he had a major crush on for years, but she never really reciprocated his feelings.

I dated a boy named Aiden during my freshman year in high school. We were the same age and in the same grade. He was funny, made me laugh, and made me feel special. Like most relationships in my life, I showed him too much affection and fell entirely too fast. I was always an intense feeler and for a girl who just wanted to feel loved and needed, I held on TIGHT to any morsel of happiness that came my way.

A few months into our relationship Aiden's parents began

expressing their concern for the fast path they felt our relationship was heading in. Having always been attached to words I expressed how strongly I felt for him at any chance I got. I was a smidge obsessed and looking back now—I know where that desperation came from. Even at 14-years-old, I was scared of losing people.

Eventually, my cute obsession translated into clinginess to Aiden, and I was crushed when he broke up with me. He was also the first African American boy to like me despite my lack of hips and ass. But the best way it seemed at the time to keep a boy was to have sex with them.

I could still vividly remember mulling over the idea of giving up my virginity to Aiden and as most teen boys did at the time, he made me feel it would've been the only thing worth staying for. That was my first true lesson in heartbreak, and it certainly would not be my last.

Many boys became crushes but my reputation of being the preacher's kid with the super strict, holier-than-thou, intimidating Caribbean parents didn't exactly make me the popular girl to date. I wasn't allowed to go to the movies, the mall, or to friends' homes who were not children of my Haitian parents' friends. I didn't attend parties or many school events.

By my sophomore year in high school, I realized the best way to get around my parents and their rules was to get a job and get involved in anything and everything I could in school. I always used the it-will-look-good-on-a-college-application excuse. After all, my parents' ultimate goal for being in this country was to provide their children with better opportunities and better access to education than they had back in Haiti.

I was never what you would call lucky in love. While other Haitian girls had wide hips, large butts, and big boobs—I unfortunately only ever fulfilled one of those categories as a teen. I always joked about being shaped like a lowercase 'p' which was my self-deprecating way of pointing out my flaws before someone else did—a habit that is now more than ever before a heavy presence in my personality.

Boys didn't like me, and I was often left struggling to find confidence in any area of my life. The black boys I liked, only liked my lighter-skinned friends. The white boys I liked were either not into me or too embarrassed to ever claim me out loud.

I longed to be chased and pursued the way boys did my friends around me who always seemed more womanly than I did. I was always the smallest and looked the youngest. The skinniest and the darkest.

In the late 90s/early 2000s era I fell nowhere on the spectrum of what was considered beautiful for Black girls like me. These insecurities hardened me in my teen years making me hyper-focused on being the absolute best at everything I did. Like always—it wasn't enough to be good. I had to be the best.

At the end of my sophomore year in high school—I was pretty serious about my extracurricular activities and was particularly excited about a club called the Scholar's Club which was historically known for being an organization amongst public high schools that gave students of color space to commune and learn how to lead within their interests. Mynoucka was the club president and I was the secretary.

Our Scholar's Club chapter included a dance team, step

team, and endless opportunities around the community and school to come together and celebrate diversity. Through this club, I grew pride in my culture and truly started to fall in love with my blackness. This was also the club Lanau and I connected through and eventually went from being bitter enemies to true friends who were slowly growing in their affection for one another.

After a loud and intense argument over what I can't for the life of me recall—we were yelling across a bus filled with our friends and club mates—one of my friends told us that we fought like an old married couple. The disgust and pure aggravation that covered our faces gets funnier with every passing year. As we recall that stupid fight of ours, I realize we were truly meant to walk this life together.

The school year continued and Lanau graduated that spring in 2004. Somehow overnight, when we got back from the trip, we realized we had no reason not to like each other and finally put down the weapons.

It was early February and Lanau was graduating the following May. Every morning he walked me to my first-period class, Music Composition and he'd later meet me after the second period to walk me to my third period, French class which happens to have been his second-period class. So, he would just hang around until I made my way upstairs to the second floor.

After he graduated and summer rolled around, we remained in contact, every so often speaking on the phone or hanging out with our mutual friends. That summer his best friend Christian started dating Mynoucka and soon most of our close friends were dating each other.

Christmas Time
1994
Asmite, Carline,
Faye & Me

Chapter 4 ~ The Start of Something New

"Take a lover who looks at you like you are a Bourbon biscuit."

~Frida Khalo

Seemingly overnight my affections for Lanau grew. He was getting ready to move to Tallahassee to start college at the historically black university (HBCU), Florida Agricultural & Mechanical University. I loved hearing about his big college plans and how he seemed to have a very clear idea as to what he wanted, where he wanted to be, and how he was going to get there.

He made everything seem possible in a very optimistic "but of course" way I'd never heard so confidently stated by a boy around my age. I was fascinated. As the days for his big college departure drew nearer, we spoke more often and began to form a different type of connection neither of us ever saw coming.

He was on his way to college, and I was smart enough to know that was not a door I wanted to open and so I held back. I was only a high schooler who had zero freedom to do as I pleased so it seemed ridiculous to me to even expect fidelity and faithfulness. The night before he left, I asked him to come over to quickly see me. Though my parents were home, for some reason it was so important for me to say goodbye to Lanau that I just told them the truth.

Something my parents often made difficult to say.

It all happened so quickly they really didn't have much time to react before I was meeting him in front of the gates of my house for a hug and to give him a letter wrapped around a tiny Bible. Yep...a Bible. Don't ask me why. At the time my faith was very important to me, and I really didn't know myself. Was the gift my way of showing I cared about him in a meaningful way? Okay—I give. Jo was young and dumb y'all!

At the start of that fall, in true Florida fashion, we were hit with one of the worst hurricanes our area had experienced since Hurricane Andrew in 1992. Hurricane Charlie of 2004 dished out a whole new level of natural disaster most kids my age had never experienced in their lifetime. The storm was so destructive it sent most college students back home to their parents, only maybe two or three weeks after the school year had officially started.

About a week later, our church tried to return to its normal activities which meant we Haitian church kids could finally see our friends after days of being trapped indoors with our parents. On a Saturday evening the youth group was gathering for its usual weekend activities. Lanau was still in town and to my surprise popped up with his friend Christian, who was there to see my friend Mynoucka who were dating each other at the time.

Bored with the church activity that night and excited to just see each other, sit and chill—we snuck out of the side door of the church and found a car hood in the parking lot to sit on and talk. As we sat there catching up, we knew something was happening between us that neither of us was comfortable with admitting out loud quite yet.

His eyes were piercing and intense with passion. In just a few short weeks of being away, I could already see the growth in who he was becoming. We spent hours outside talking about everything and nothing at all. It felt good to sit near him and feel the warmth of his body. We flirted but I still couldn't tell if he was just being polite to his still-in-high-school kid friend, or if he felt something in return. Something for sure had changed and I wanted to know how he felt.

When I got home later that night, I called Mynoucka and told her what I was feeling. She didn't seem surprised and thought it was worth pursuing. The next morning while hanging halfway through a church window—I told him I had feelings for him, and he expressed he felt the same way. I wish I could say that this was some romantic transaction between two people, but it was far clumsier as his friends and my friends went back and forth, verbally baiting each other while dropping heavy hints that Lanau and I had feelings for one another.

Mynoucka, Faye, Gertrude and I were youth ministry teachers for all the kids in our church that were 12 and under. Every Sunday morning we'd lead them in fun, children-friendly praise and worship. We planned lessons, games, snacks, movies and even performances like singing and dancing. Every few months or so, or during holidays, the girls and I hosted Sunday evening recitals and youth-led services which allowed parents to see what their kids were learning while they attended traditional church services. The group was called Good News for Kids. Our services were held in a different space within the church that gave us access to windows and doors apart from the watchful eyes of the adults in the congregation. During some services we brought the kids outside to play and have some fun.

At the end of church that fateful Sunday of confessions, I met Lanau outside of his car in the parking lot. Wracked with nerves that he actually had feelings for me, and knew I had feelings for him, my teen mind struggled to remain calm. To this day I could not for the life of me remember what words we exchanged in that interaction. All I could vividly remember doing was giving him a quick hug, kissing him on the mouth, and running away like the true idiot I felt like in that mortifying moment.

I fully expected to get home and receive a call about how weird he thought I was, and that he could never date me and my childish ways. Instead, he called to tell me how surprised he was at what was happening between us and that he never believed I could ever like him.

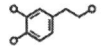

The following October he escorted me to my homecoming dance and for the first time, I felt all those special feelings I always wished to have. Lanau popped up in town for a surprise visit or sent me detailed emails of how he felt and what he wanted out of life. He made me feel important and worthy.

Our first real date started with one of these surprise drop-ins and after what felt like forever since I'd seen him—I completely swooned when he showed up at my job as a cashier at HomeGoods. Jumping into his arms with a burst of pure joy I'd never felt—seeing him, touching him, and holding him, felt like an out-of-body experience. His smile alone made my knees weak and I had never felt more wanted. We quickly made plans to get together after my shift was over as we reluctantly parted ways.

Later that evening, he picked me up in his dad's red pickup

truck and we drove to a nearby park in downtown Fort Myers that overlooked the bay and had a pier overlooking the water that had us entranced from the very start. Dressed in a black tank top that I stole from Carline's closet I felt grown. The top was a sleeveless, low-cut, V-neck with a black string that crisscrossed and laced up my cleavage. I paired it with a pair of fitted flared dark wash jeans that kept Lanau's hands exactly where I'd wanted them all night long.

Sitting on the pier beyond the rocks—though we were surrounded by beauty with the city lights bouncing off the ocean that whooshed back and forth beneath us, we remained focused on us. He looked at me like no boy had ever done before in 17 years of life and I knew he was falling just as hard as I was.

Lanau made me feel like a woman. He held me in just the right way and kissed me every time like it was our absolute last. His eyes sent electric currents rushing through my body in a way I could barely stand to contain. Neither of us had experienced growing love and passion, and I wanted more and more of him.

We were addicted to one another and there, started the fusing of our souls in such a profound way we were yet to fully understand. All I knew for certain was that I was in love and he loved me back just as fiercely.

Months went by and we only told our friends we were "talking"—whatever the hell that meant. From what I could tell back then, it was that transitional time at the start of a romantic relationship where you were still unsure if you wanted to be officially boyfriend and girlfriend. Even as a teen myself, I struggled to understand what the different levels of dating were or meant.

Being with Lanau was freeing. For the first time in my life, I was with someone who genuinely saw me, for me. We spoke on the phone nonstop and he would go out of his way to buy phone cards so we could still communicate off our ancient, bulky cell phones and maintain our long-distance relationship. He challenged me to think harder and to stretch my mind further into deeper understanding.

I was used to downplaying my intelligence or what many viewed as nerdiness around boys but those were the very things Lanau loved about me and found attractive. Not at all annoying or lame as I had led myself to believe most of my life. He listened as I shared stories and details from books I'd read, things I've researched and he'd challenge me to take in the complexities of the world that was present around me.

For hours Lanau spoke enthusiastically about politics, our government, and the states of our society's social constructs. I fell in love with his mind and thought he was and still is the most beautiful human mind I have ever had the pleasure of knowing.

On the evening of January 31st, 2005, Lanau told me he loved me for the first time. I remember it well because I was in the bathroom of our Atlanta hotel room on the same annual Scholar's Club trip where we had our very open, awkward marital (lol) argument when we were on our way back home from just one year before.

Lanau came home to see me the weekend before Valentine's Day. We had just spent the day together and were on the phone that evening soaking up the excitement and passion that bubbled around us. Listening to India Arie's Voyage to India album a song came on in a moment of silence between the two of us. As the melody danced in the air, the lyrics captured my attention...

> *"It's like yesterday,*
> *I didn't even know your name,*
> *Now today, you're always on my mind.*
> *I never could have predicted that I'd feel this way,*
> *You are a beautiful surprise..."*

I turned the music up and told him to just listen.

"Intoxicated every time I hear your voice,
You've got me on a natural high.
It's almost like I didn't even have a choice
You are a beautiful surprise.

Whatever it is that you came to teach me,
I am here to learn it cause,
I believe that we are written in the stars,
And I don't know what the future holds
But I'm here at the moment
And I'm thankful for the man that you are..."

The lyrics connected us and in a way that we knew was uniquely our story. A couple hours later, before the sun even came up, we met up at our special spot by the pier. Parked beneath the bridge, we listened to the song over and over again while holding each other tightly. I was in love with my best friend, and I knew we were written in the stars.

A couple of days later, right after Valentine's Day, Lanau had his friend deliver a cereal box that was actually a greeting card that contained a copy of my favorite book The Wind Blows Backward by Mary Downing Hahn, Alicia Key's CD Diary, and T.I.'s Urban Legend CD. It was the sweetest most thoughtful gift anyone had ever given me.

That same week, he asked me to officially be his girlfriend. We giggled the whole time realizing we'd never actually had that conversation and I thought it was super cute. I couldn't have been happier to accept.

Our Wedding Day
June 8, 2013

L & Jo
The Early Years

Chapter 5 ~ I Came Out of the Womb Winding My Hips!

"Well, I hope that if you are out there and read this and that, yes, it's true, I'm here, no I'm just as strange as you."

~Frida Khalo

Call it the Caribbean in me but I've always LOVED dancing. The day I discovered my hips—it was over. The first real dancing I watched was amongst my Haitian community. Whether we were at a wedding reception, a house party, or even at some church or school-related events—I've always been mesmerized by our variations of dancing like Zouk and Kompa.

Zouk dancing is typically celebratory, fast paced, and rich in history, traditions, storytelling and even patriotism. This is the type of music you'll hear at street carnivals like on our flag day, May 18. Sometimes the women performing these dances adorn themselves in elaborate costumes with feathers, face-paints, and jewels.

In simpler settings where stories and history are being shared amongst families, friends, and neighbors—the dancer instead may choose to wear a simple handmade traditional dress.

Kompa is the most popular form of dancing in the Haitian culture. Whether you're listening to the radio, at a club, or a party—Kompa music is playing, and make no mistake—

SOMEONE will be moving their hips! Kompa is a sensual couples dance that is meant to bring people together. Haiti's version of "pop music," songs could be about love, sex, relationships, sorrows, break ups or even just altogether thought-provoking.

A proud, long-winded, hella-extra bunch, we tend to be culturally—this is even more obvious in our music which could range anywhere from six to damn-near ten minutes long! Invite us to your simple backyard gathering and just mind ya bidness when you see us coming through with a beat face, fresh hairstyles and a gown or two to change into! What can I say? Our thespian ways are an art form, a religion—it's a lifestyle y'all!

You cannot experience the full cultural-pull of the Haitian lifestyle, if you've yet to gyrate (gouyad), pelvis to pelvis with someone during a party! The wildly talented, singer, comedian, personality and true Haitian Queen, Jessie Woo didn't sing "Party like Haitians" in her hit song Vacation for nothing!

RANDOM FACT: The Citadel—proper name Citadelle Laferrière, is a large mountaintop fortress located in Northern Haiti. Built in the 19th century by the order of Haitian Revolutionary Henri Christophe, it was important for defense for the newly independent country. Built by tens of thousands of former slaves, The Citadel is the largest fortress in the Western hemisphere. And fun fact: it's also where the aforementioned Haitian American artist filmed the music video!

At 17, I attended the wedding of a family friend with my mom. Lanau and I just started dating a couple of months before that so no adults in my life knew about our relationship yet. He also attended the wedding and though my mom was not cool with me dating—she knew I could not resist a good Kompa jam. So, when Alan Cave's Se Pa Pou Dat came on I made my way to the dance floor, and as if he knew I'd be there, Lanau met me in the middle of the crowded floor.

It was the first time I danced Kompa with a boy. Everything and everyone in that room melted away, and it was just him and me. I'd never had anyone hold me like that. Moved with me like that—as if our bodies were now one. That look in his eyes put a spell on me. It wasn't until the song faded to the end did I notice we had cleared the dance floor, as the whole room watched. Little did I know I'd spend a lifetime clearing the dance floor with him!

On the way home my mom asked me, "Who taught you how to dance like that?" Impressed she noticed, I smiled and said, "Who do you think?!" Even in the darkness of the night's drive home, I could see the smile spread across her face.

FUN FACT: I used to be a competitive ballroom dancer! In the Spring of 2005, I was itching to just try something new. Couldn't tell you what came over me but one day I just walked into a random ballroom dance studio that was not far from my house. I'd done all kinds of dancing throughout my life, even going to a performing arts high school; I was given many opportunities to explore different art forms. Though I majored in strings, having played the violin from 6th grade all the way through high school—it was something I mostly did because my parents liked it and my best friend was also part of the orchestra. But ballroom dancing was different and something I'd never seen anyone doing. From the moment I took my first dance lesson I was hooked. I competed for almost four years locally in South Florida, before I had to choose between it and completing college. Still—it was one of the best times of my life and I hope one day return to the d

This should go without saying at this point in case you've continued to miss the "subtle" hints—I love being Haitian. The music, the food, the storytelling, the art and overall vivaciousness of our culture is like no other—in my entirely humble and honest opinion. I can still remember once waking up early in the morning and catching my mom and dad amid an intimate kompa dance as they floated around the kitchen completely lost in each other's eyes. I marveled at the way my mother's hips whined and swayed while my father's arms wrapped around her effortlessly like a silk ribbon. I dreamed about doing the same someday with my husband. At Lanau and my house today, that's just called Thursday.

Having so much pride in my Haitian heritage—as a child growing up in the 90s in Florida, I struggled to understand why Americans (predominantly African American) kids would often make fun of us. It was typical on any given day to be asked if your family ate cats and dogs, or why did your parents dress funny or had an accent. It was one of the first forms of bullying I experienced in my life, and it affected the way I looked at myself and my community for years to come.

The mainstream media's understanding of what Haiti and Haitian culture looks like has always been from the perspective of the colonizer. I can remember feeling hurt and angry when kids would say that Haiti and Haitian people were dirty, smelly and poor. They imagine our world to be nothing but scarcely dressed children with bloated bellies from eating mud pies and being malnourished. On the contrary—the Haiti I know and experienced with my family who were of the island could not be more different.

Haiti is rich with culture. Brilliant, powerful-minded people who possessed an ancestral pride and passion in who they knew themselves to be—not at all what the world saw of them or thought they understood. As my school years became more permanently bound in Florida, so did the bullies that regularly made fun of me. They were usually Black American girls who despised me for simply being me. Too "white," too small, too squeaky, too goody-goody, etc. As I got further into my teen years, my bullies came from all backgrounds. Whether it was the mostly White, rich beach kids, the kids in the hood, or even other Haitian kids who joined the ranks of "bully or be bullied."

RANDOM RANT: Being so much smaller than most kids my age, I felt gave people the idea that I was easy to push around—a notion that many mistakenly make today. But Jo is all grown up now and will not hesitate to read you for filth using jargon you've never heard outside of a Sylvia Plath novel!

At the end of the day, I'd then go to my beautifully kept and yes, a bit eccentric home—on account of my traditional Haitian mother's unique taste and obsession with figurines, plastic chair coverings, clear carpet runners, beaded curtains in every entrance and silk flowers—we did live well. I knew our home was weird. It was overly clean due to my mother's compulsive need to clean daily and fill the house with the smell of a rather hard-hitting mixture of Fabuloso and Clorox bleach. If you were not faint from the "cleanliness" a mere four steps into the house then, my dear, our home was not quite clean enough for my mother's liking.

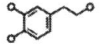

Because of the ridiculous attitudes and stereotypes towards the Haitian community growing up in Florida, a lot of Haitian kids—out of fear of being picked on or physically attacked, and/or harassed, would simply conform to the more acceptable African American vernacular and social attitudes. There were kids that were born in Haiti who still had their accent who would pass it off as a Jamaican accent—which most people thought was much cooler than other Caribbean people.

Even understanding the fear and pressure to just be "normal"—it always irked me to see kids I went to church with pretty much every damn night of the week, including weekends, would spend their school days putting on an act and joining in on the bullying of their fellow Haitian peers. As kids we all take our own paths. Many of those kids back then are now my friends on social media and have since become rather loud and proud about their Haitian identity.

I couldn't do it though. I thought back to the day I came home from second grade after Sasha Robinson asked me in front of our entire class on the playground, "Why you talk so white?!" The twisted look on her face as she said it made me feel horrible. I spoke with proper annunciation because all my American culture, reading, and language came from white characters. In the 90s there were not many Black celebrities to identify with. I didn't know this was a thing until I was confronted with it. It would remain an insecurity of mine for most of my life.

RANDOM FACT: Did you know the United States didn't recognize Haiti as an independent nation until 1862?! That's how corrupt, twisted and arrogant we are in this country. Only a whining toddler on the world stage in comparison to other nations and it took us 58 years to even acknowledge our existence as a free Black people. Of course, when you're still in the process of using Black human bodies as slaves to build your country—you can't possibly be bothered with insignificant things like "freedom" and "independence." And still till this day America's political noose around Haiti's neck only tightens with time. Let's be clear, America has only kinda sorta abolished slavery in the states. We fail to mention or recognize the grip of death they have on people beyond its borders.

My parents were very proud of their accomplishments despite starting out with nothing. They worked arduously to get to a place where they owned a home, had vehicles, and other things of value they once could not even dream of. I always imagine what it must've been like to leave everything they knew back home at a really young age—trading their culture and country for 40-hour work weeks and working multiple jobs all in the name of the "American Dream." Whether for themselves or living vicariously through their children, all they wanted was a life with options and opportunities.

My father immigrated in the late 70s and brought my mother in with him in 1983 after having my sister, who is four years older than me, in St. Marten. People don't realize how fortunate we are to have access to cold fridges and fresh foods already stored and ready for our next meals.

My parents never wanted me to be complacent in my privilege as an American-raised kid. My mom talked about what it was like to be left in complete poverty when her father died—leaving my grandmother with 12 children she now had the sole responsibility of raising on her own.

My mom told us stories of having to wake up before dawn just to go down to the ocean every morning to fetch the water supply for the family's first part of the day. Being one of the oldest my mom and her sister before her, carried large pails and tubs of water. Only to head back out moments later to go fetch their food for the day.

My dad was the son of farmers whose lives took a complete turn after my grandmother passed away from stomach cancer, leaving behind my eight-year-old father and his twin sisters. Watching his wife die slowly over the course of several months sent my grandfather over the edge, and he just never recovered.

Becoming a virtual recluse, he spent the rest of his life drinking himself into a stupor, speaking to himself incessantly, droning on for days at a time about random things that hardly ever made sense. As he grew older my dad paid for people who lived in his old village to look after him. Grandpa refused the notion of ever leaving the place where his beloved died.

Though my dad rarely spoke about him, especially after his death, I could tell he felt shame around his father's condition. From the moment his mother passed away, despite being a little boy himself, he committed to taking care of his sisters and still does today, regardless of where my aunts are in their lives.

I always admired his loyalty to them and can't help but wonder how he allowed my sisters and I to grow so far apart—oftentimes, being the separator himself as we became adults.

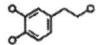

Growing up in a completely different world than my parents were raised in stacked several barriers between us as I got older. They worked hard and really didn't have the option to take time for themselves or even be mindful of their parenting. The roles in my household often muddled between parent and child. It also took us in and out of childhood regularly.

One day you could be getting yelled at for that one phone call they received from a teacher informing them of your bad behaviors like talking too much in class. And the next day you are their English translator, reading letters sent in the mail—bills, financial statements. My sister and I often translated for them when they'd go to the bank, post office, doctor's office and pretty much anywhere they needed more than basic English words and phrases to get by. I regularly gave them crash-courses in American small-talk to help them in their daily travels.

My dad was pretty social. He enjoyed starting random conversations with people in lines at the store, the gas station—just about anywhere. He was naturally funny although his, a bit, too-kind demeanor often got him stuck in conversations where he was barely understanding ten percent of what he was being told. Regardless, he was always courteous and nodded A LOT and occasionally threw in an "Mmm hmmm. Okay. Yes, my fren."

I went with my dad on a bank trip once because it was in the mall, and there was a high chance that he'd make me smile from ear to ear after I'd patiently get through his boring banking—he'd sometimes let me go into a store and buy something. This particular bank trip, however, remains engraved in my memory.

We walked into the brightly standard-looking bank and took our place at the end of the line of customers waiting to see the teller. I don't think I was more than 11 at the time when I noticed the tone and disrespectful way my father was addressed once it was our turn to approach the available teller. Ignoring her rude tone or maybe just being used to it at this point, my dad went on to explain that something was wrong on his monthly bank statement, and he just wanted to come in and have it corrected. He brought all his paperwork and receipts with him to further explain. By now, my dad was a U.S. citizen and had taken night classes to improve English. So, he really didn't need much assistance for basic transactions.

Cutting off my dad before he finished his explanation, the teller rolled her eyes at him and said, "Sir, if you don't speak English, I can't help you!" My dad kept his composure noticing the attitude right away and tried to explain in a different way. The teller put her hand up as if to shut him up and repeated slowly and louder, "Sir... if... you... don't... speak... English... then..."

Noticing the stares from people around us, I spoke up and cut her off, speaking sternly, "Excuse me, my dad isn't deaf, slow, or stupid. You don't need to talk him like that! If you can't help him then find someone who can without being rude!"

A manager must've overheard me and came over right away to handle the situation after apologizing to us profusely. As I grew older, I interjected myself into more moments like these with my parents. I knew how many people viewed Haitians and foreigners in general in America. It was a constant reminder that certain people always treated us badly regardless of how kind and composed we are. Even then, I could not stand just doing nothing when I saw others get treated unfairly because of their differences.

My First Ballroom Dancing Competition

Chapter 6 ~Daddy's Girl

"Pain, pleasure and death are no more than a process for existence. The revolutionary struggle in this process is a doorway to open intelligence."

~Frida Khalo

Like so many other times in my life, I turned to writing when a sudden work-related accident left my father paralyzed from the waist down. I wrote the following story a few years after the incident happened. I was in sixth grade. This was my very first piece of writing to be publicly published in a small-town publication in Fort Myers, Florida. It also won first place in a writing contest my language arts teacher secretly submitted my story to, and I felt so proud to be chosen.

A Useless Wish

As a little girl, my father used to read me several stories about the most extravagant princes and princesses, genies in bottles and witches. In some of these stories, the characters were granted wishes or even recited certain poems to make their dreams come true. And as a child, I listened closely and hung onto every word. But while putting me to bed or getting me ready for that tragic trip to the doctor's, daddy never explained how these things came about. Why did every character in these books get what they wanted through spells, wishes, and magic?

Every child is naïve and vulnerable to some and maybe all teachings. However, when these beliefs and stories fall through, we are stripped of our innocence and left amid a shattered dream.

I was one of these dreamers. I believed in Santa Claus and the tooth fairy and even clicking my heels three times to reach my desired destination. After all, this was possible in all the books and TV shows. Why not dream? Why not wish? And most importantly, why not believe?

Growing up, my father and I had a very close relationship. For as long as I can remember, he would always refer to me as his Little Jo. I was daddy's little girl, and nobody could tell me differently. Daddy and I, along with mommy and my sister Carline, lived in a small urban neighborhood, in the center of Asbury Park, New Jersey. The year was 1993 and I had just entered the first grade.

One evening I sat anxiously in my bedroom awaiting my father's arrival. It was later than usual this evening and even though I couldn't tell the time yet, I knew this because it was becoming darker outside.

A couple of hours later, I heard the roaring of daddy's engine pulling into the driveway. Without hesitation, I leaped out of my bed and made my way to the hot and humid garage. The place was pungent with the intense smell of gasoline; a scent I never really adapted to. As he opened the car door and stepped out of the rickety, old, pale blue truck, I jumped on him. He smiled at me awkwardly but behind his smile was a cringing look of pain. He hugged me tightly and put me down.

Confused, I watched as he limped through the garage doors

and into the family room. I figured he was just being funny and didn't think much of it after that. Daddy was always trying to humor us.

After we had dinner that night, just a few minutes later from behind the walls of my bedroom, I heard a capricious sound coming from the bathroom. I uneasily walked out into the hall and pressed my ear up against the bathroom door. I couldn't make anything out but as the sound grew disturbingly louder and louder, I was terrified.

It was my dad! He sounded as if he was choking! Panic-stricken, I burst into the bathroom, and to my surprise; my father stood there, lunged forward with a peculiar, thick crimson, fluid hacking up through his mouth.

"MOMMY! Come quick! Daddy is puking bloody stuff!" I hollered out in astonishment. My mother came charging in with my sister following.

My mom broke into a hysterical shriek as she threw her arms over my father's bare back. Dumbfounded, I stood there helpless and confounded at the sight before me.

Everything after that happened so fast that I was unable to comprehend it all. An ambulance showed up with its raging lights flickering on and off—it went from blue to white, to red, and back again. The piercing sound of sirens made my stomachache. My heart was beating a thousand miles per second and I felt a faint headache come over me. Men and women in uniforms invaded our home, shouting, rustling, and moving quickly throughout the house. Equipment was thrown around, left and right and all I could see was daddy's frightened face looking back at me. A look I had never seen before on him.

When we arrived at the hospital, doctors and nurses bombarded the vehicle shouting strange codes and words that I didn't understand. I watched confusingly, as they all pinched, pricked, and poked at my father's still body.

As I entered the automatic glass doors, a nurse with bright red hair and blue eyes took me by the hand and led me away from all the panic. I cried out to my mother to come and get me but she didn't even notice through all the commotion.

Inside a crowded room, I was told to take a seat near a messy pile of raggedy, old magazines. I looked around at the people mourning and weeping and then it suddenly all clicked to me. I had seen this scene before on TV shows. In front of me, an old lady held her granddaughter tightly as she gasped for air. To my left, a man pressed a white rag to his heart, bleeding uncontrollably.

I was startled and thought I had to be dreaming. How come so many people were in so much pain around me? Why was daddy bleeding clots through his mouth? None of it made sense. Daddy was always so magnanimous and courageous. Like the characters in the stories, he read to me. He was brave. How can something like this happen to him?

All of a sudden, I was smothered by my thoughts and questions. I felt claustrophobic, I had to get out. Without a second thought, I rushed out of the hospital doors, into the cool, damp night air. Beyond the parking lot, there was a white bench that sat before some bushes. I took a seat and buried my tear-drenched face into the palms of my hands. I didn't understand this. Nobody in my family had ever been sick before—at least not seriously. Why now? Were we cursed or did we have bad luck?

In the distance, frogs and crickets joined in a harmony of

croaking and chirping. The background sounds of the wind and rustling leaves on the pavement battling in a whirl of motion sent chills down my back. The beautiful colors of the night sky took my breath away as I looked up at all the diamond-like stars.

My thoughts brought me back to school when I had learned how to recite that poem when making a wish. I observed the blackness above me and searched for that bright star that illuminated the somber darkness. When I had found it, I shut my eyes, watertight, and recited the famous lines:

"Starlight, star bright..." I figured that maybe, just maybe, my father would be all right, if only I wished he would. Everything would go back to normal.

The next morning, we went home but daddy stayed at the hospital. Later on at home, Mom came into my room explaining how things were going to be different from now on at home. Mom continued and explained how daddy was going to need an operation.

I was very angry because I couldn't understand why my wish hadn't worked. Instead of everything getting better, they became worse. I made them worse.

Two weeks later, daddy was home and recovering from his tragic accident. The mystery was finally solved. My dad worked in a factory that produced material for building things such as roads and things of that nature. A very large box filled with this stuff was dropped from 16 feet high above the ground onto my dad's back at work. This caused his spine to be completely crippled and horrifically damaged. The doctors said his chances of ever walking again were slim to none.

After the accident, daddy and I spent several hours a day together. Doing nothing just being close to him put my mind at ease. I was scared he wouldn't love me anymore if I told him about my messing up the wish—that I was the reason why he was still hurt. So I kept it to myself. I didn't want to risk losing daddy. I never stopped trying though. Every night I recited the poem and every morning things were exactly as they were the day before.

Two months from the incident, Mom and Carline went shopping and I volunteered to stay at home with daddy. He spent most of his days in bed and a wheelchair when he grew tired of lying down. As I was walking past his bedroom one evening, I poked my head through the crack and was shocked when I saw him lying there helpless with a stream of tears falling down his cheeks. It was heart-wrenching to see him so down and I remembered what he'd sometimes do for me when I was sad.

Hoping to cheer him up, I brought into his bedroom our favorite father-daughter tape with the song "Butterfly Kisses" by Michael W. Smith on it. I popped it into the tape player and asked daddy for a dance. He laughed hysterically as I did my best to keep a straight face. "May I have this dance, monsieur?"

Still a little feeble, he took my hand and stood up for the first time, in what seemed like an eternity, and danced with me. I spent the rest of the day playing and joking around with him. And when the moment presented itself, I was courageous and told him about my failed wish. He laughed a little and looked at me in the eye and said, "No wish is gonna fix me baby, you just have to pray and be brave."

From that moment on I realized that my life would never be the same. I wouldn't always be daddy's little girl. I was growing up and the safety of my ignorance was rapidly crumbling around me. I realized at the tender age of six, that you can't just wish your problems away—you have to face them head-on.

Today my father has prevailed over his injury and has lived a full and meaningful life. Having several limitations to his physical abilities, my dad is unable to work legally and now owns a Caribbean produce store, Edouard's Retail in Fort Myers. He went to ministry school and went from being our church deacon to a pastor.

My dad has said that he doesn't regret his accident because he feels it has led him to a greater place. Before, he worked all day—almost every day, and had no time to really go after his dreams or spend time with his family.

His setbacks allowed him to become a better man, not just for himself but for our family. My father still suffers from frequent back and leg problems as a result but has been walking for years without the aid of a wheelchair or a cane. He shows no visible signs of being disabled and has seen the most success in his life, after his accident—and neither luck nor wish can ever work such miracles.

Reading this story now brings tears to my eyes because I realize how much trauma and anxiety I was navigating as a little girl. For the longest time my child-mind was convinced I had done something and that's why my dad was suffering. This also takes me back to when my relationship with my father was strong and we knew each other inside and out.

He was always protective of all of us, and I think when I

was younger it was easier to meet my needs and making me happy was easier. But growing isn't easy and I couldn't help that my body was changing and so was I.

As I grew into my teen years and began my menstrual cycle—my mom made it a point to break down that playful, fun, and open relationship dad and I shared. She lectured me about being more modest, dressing in private and even told me I was too old to be sitting on his lap or snuggling up with him.

I imagine she had a similar discussion with my dad because we were never again the same. We grew apart and I became more closed-off feeling like I no longer had that dad I could tell anything to and just be light-hearted with. After a while, watching me grow became uncomfortable for him to the point where it often felt like he stopped trying to even know me at all.

I kept up with the activities I did at church like singing and dancing with my friends Mynoucka, Gertrude and Faye— in an all-girls gospel group we called "Heavenly Stars" which is a name we adapted from my dad's fancy French translation which I just remember including the word "étoiles." Our young minds could not truly appreciate then, as we probably would think about it today—nah. It still sounded bougie as fuck!

My dad enjoyed his early role of playing our "manager!" Listen, y'all don't laugh! At First Haitian Baptist of Fort Myers—we had lofty goals and were forever ambitious. I could also blame this on the movie, Selena, that my dad and I may have watched one too many times.

RANDOM RANT: Why will our parents watch a movie over and over again for like a week straight?! And will still ask you questions throughout the entire movie they're practically reciting the lines to. I'm convinced my parents were the ones who ruined The Titanic for me. But I digress…

I would say this is about the time the chase for my dad's affections and approval started. The hugs, kisses and snuggles decreased and my desperation to remain connected to my daddy only increased.

By the time I got married, we were complete strangers to another, and he was disappointed when I wouldn't allow him any control in my love life. Ever since I was a kid, he would tell me if I didn't allow him and my mother to choose who, when and how I began dating and then married—that I would never be in a successful marriage—Yeah, it sounded insane to me too even as a kid. My dad and I just stopped speaking the same language and he became more hardened toward me, just like my mother always had been.

These are the little comforts my writing has brought me throughout my life—just giving me the ability to not just capture memories with a photograph. I can capture the story behind who we were in those memories. It's my superpower and I think deep down—I always knew it.

Chapter 7 ~ Once Upon These Days

"Can verbs be made up? I'll tell you one. I heaven you, so my wings will open wide to love you boundlessly. I am not sick. I am broken. But I am happy to be alive as long as I can paint."

~Frida Khalo

Lanau and I had been enjoying and indulging in our first few months as a couple. Everything was new, exciting and we were in constant awe of the fact that our perceptions of one another before we began dating were so off.

We spoke religiously over the phone. Umm, correction: We spoke religiously over my blue, LED MetroPCS Nokia cellphone which was the early 2000s first cell phone starter kit. Lanau had a college dorm room telephone. As a freshman on campus, he was limited to not having a car. Still, almost daily he would hike the long-distance, in the chilly Tallahassee night air, all the way off-campus to purchase a phone card from a gas station to call me every night. He eventually got himself a red Samsung flip phone—which was likely one of the first of its kind! Ha!

I can still remember begging my dad to go to the store with me to buy one since I was too young to sign any paperwork. Of course, my dad was not exactly elated that I wanted to get a cell. By that point, he was in a fierce, overly protective father mode.

I convinced him that it was an essential purchase now that I was driving myself everywhere, was working, was in multiple after-school activities that often ran late and worked at the church doing youth ministries on the weekends. In reality, I simply didn't want to worry about my parents eavesdropping on my calls since seeing, speaking, or even breathing near a boy in our household was strictly forbidden.

Back then ringtones were still a thing and my stomach fluttered with butterflies every time Lanau's assigned ringtone *Always Be My Baby* by Mariah Carey came on. *Sweet Thang* by Chaka Khan was his for my calls. We loved to belt it out terribly when we were in the car together and laughed uncontrollably at our mutual cheesiness.

We remained connected at all times and I loved how attentive he was to me, even though I was in college more than six hours away. Whether we were emailing, calling, texting, or sending things to each other, I loved how much he doted on me, asked me what I was thinking, and just truly wanted to know the girl behind the mask. He was sweet and taught me it was okay to let others in.

Opening up at first was challenging. Being a sheltered kid with only a handful of real friends, I wasn't used to someone being genuinely interested in what I had to say—especially a boy. Guys weren't exactly lining up at my locker so even though the attention was overwhelming at first, he kept reassuring me it was okay to stop thinking and allow myself to fall.

I'd never met someone so confident, knew where they were going to be and exactly how he planned to get there. Standing at about five feet and six inches, his presence, and energy alone made him six feet tall. He always seemed to have it all together and would encourage me to discuss anything either of us was feeling. "We should never go to bed, angry baby. I'm always here to listen to you," he would say.

His affirmations and genuine words helped me grow from the child he'd met to the grown and confident woman he knew was before him all along. He found beauty in my vulnerabilities and made me feel safe to let go.

During times he was struggling to buy food, I would have such a good time putting together boxes of college care packages and would send his favorite snacks, food, toiletries, and medicine for the headaches he often got from days of pulling all-nighters or barely having time to eat. We took pride in the little things we were able to do for one another.

With Lanau, I became a different kind of me. He did more than make me feel special, he helped me gain the courage to show the world who I was. The intensity of the way he would look me in the eye made me swoon, feeling like I was the prettiest girl in the world.

He too was also a better version of himself when he was with me, and I knew our connection ran deeper than even we had allowed ourselves to say out loud. We knew each other in a way no one around us, not our friends or even our families could attest to. We never ran out of things to talk about, and I'm never not surprised by the fact that we can still talk about anything and everything. Our ambition and hunger for building our success aligned that I knew would someday change our lives.

With us both being the child of first-generation immigrants, we knew the immense pressure our parents were putting on us. It was never enough to just do your best—you had to be the best. Also being the youngest of our siblings we connected over the inconsistencies of Haitian parenting that so easily could destroy any ounce of love, confidence, and self-esteem you have in yourself.

He understood when I wasn't allowed to be out at night or go to parties because of the dungeon I was metaphorically locked in by the "'rents." Up until I was with Lanau, no boys ever hung around very long once they knew what my parents were like. Lanau was just different. He wasn't easily spooked or phased by anything. I especially loved it when he'd just roll with the punches when every date practically came with an elaborate cover story, several phone calls to friends, and a decoy!

By year three, he was a pro at climbing gates, scaling fences, ducking, crawling, and practically slithering his way into the house, remaining low to avoid any motion sensors that could set off our alarm. Looking back now, I can't believe we were bold enough to pull such schemes. If my dad had woken up just once during one of those sneak-ins, I cannot even fathom what would have happened to us both. But Lanau was worth it and made me fearless.

Lanau was happy to be home for the summer of 2005. Attending the prominent business administration program at one of the top HBCUs in Tallahassee—Florida Agricultural & Mechanical University better known as, "FAAAAAMUUU!"

He loved it there. I could SEE him growing there. He left

home with basic little boy dreams and came back a man ready to take the world by storm—even more confident and sure of himself than I'd ever seen him before. Many of us battle with the person we are versus the person we want to be. Lanau taught me that it wasn't necessary to collect the opinions of who you ought to be when no one on that planet knows your innermost thoughts and desires.

Coming from a family who really loved their routine and rarely swayed from it, I was never taught the art of opening up and sharing my feelings. In our home, feelings, doubts, fears, or worries were simply weaknesses. Their idea? Fake it till you make it!

Though we had spent countless hours on the phone talking about how we missed each other, when Lanau came home that summer he realized the barriers, barbed wire, and electric fence that stood between us with my strict parents and my working hard to be able to spend those days with him.

By the end of Spring 2005, Lanau decided to come home for the summer because he was homesick and missed his friends. As far as what others thought of our relationship—they believed he was just with me for the sex or some sort of conquest of the preacher's good little girl. It hurt to know that no one believed me, let alone, believed I was capable of handling myself with a boy who was only two years older. I was a devoted church girl who always had an infinity to lead and to create. And just as I write these words, I realized I've been a creator my whole life.

The Call That Changed Everything

At the end of the summer of 2005, my world came crashing down around me. Lanau's ex-girlfriend got pregnant over the summer when he was home visiting. Up until this point, our relationship was pure bliss, and we were standing the test of time, well at least for being in our late teens. I was set to start my senior year in high school that fall and was nowhere near prepared for what was about to hit me.

It was early fall, and I was being recognized by the school board and superintendent for the success of my teen to young elementary schools' Teen Trendsetters program. I ushered this chapter into our school district, alongside Mynoucka, the prior school year.

Teen Trendsetters was a program in which high school students would take on the task of tutoring struggling first, second, and third-grade readers within our local elementary schools. So about once a week, I and a team of students that we trained and qualified for the program would be assigned a student to work with every few months, or as long as each child needed. The program was so successful that it caught the attention of the county's school board officials.

On this particular evening, I was invited to accept my award and was told I could bring someone special to attend alongside me, so I invited Lanau. It was about 7pm that evening when we were attending the school board award ceremony.

After a fairly quick and smooth ceremony, Lanau and I decided to run to K-Mart, for what I think was a cover folder for a written assignment that I had due in school the next day. As we walked out of the store, my 2006 Metro PCS, blue and grey Nokia cell phone buzzed over and over again until we'd settled back in my silver Toyota Corolla. Still, in the parking lot of the local K-Mart, I answered what eventually became a call. With Lanau next to me, I answered the phone.

"Hello?"

"Is this Josette, Lanau's girlfriend?"

"Um, yeah...," sounding perplexed. "Who is this?" I asked.

"That's not important. Did he tell you he's got a baby on the way?!" said the unfamiliar voice.

Looking over at Lanau, I ask, "What?! Who is this?!" The line clicked and the phone disconnected.

Lanau asked me what was wrong and who was on the phone.

"It was a girl. She said you had a baby on the way."

"What?!" He looked just as confused as I was. "That was probably one of those prank calls" At 18, and still very, very naïve, I believed him and we drove to his house in silence. A couple more times the calls came and the caller hang up as soon as I answered. By the time we were pulling into his driveway, in front of his parents' house, Lanau seemed uneasy, and I knew something was not right.

Another call came through this time, I answered the call and the voice on the other end was once again unfamiliar, but it was different from the previous call. She said her name was Meghan and that she was two months pregnant with Lanau's baby. Looking at Lanau, I repeated the words out loud. By the lifeless look that fell over his face, I knew she was right.

I think this was the very first time I had felt true heartbreak. As the news cleared up and spread to his parents who were inside the house that evening, I found myself standing outside of myself. It hurt so bad. I had never felt such betrayal and it was hard to imagine the same soul who had spent the last year of my life revolutionizing it, was just that soon, tearing my heart apart. This was also the first time I saw Lanau cry, and I knew he was truly sorry for the hell he had unleashed on my innocent and unsuspecting heart.

That evening seemed to have flown by like a hurricane and just the same as any other night, I drove home, walked into my house, kissed my parents 'hello' who were already tucked in bed, and locked myself in my bedroom, crying inconsolably until the next morning.

Someone That I Used to Know

In February of 2006, the true reality of my relationship with Lanau slapped me in the most humiliating public forum. I was a dual-enrollment student in college while completing junior and senior year in high school.

At this point, most of my classes were at the college so just as it was important to me to be active in school affairs and organizations—it was even more essential to me at Edison State College (the name at the time), to be a leader and to learn to be more confident in what I had to say and offer.

I'd just joined the Haitian American Student Initiative club which was an on-campus organization led by one of my friends Jean, who is better known today as Dr. Jean Williamceau! Having been more vocal at the recent meetings, a few other Student Government Association members and I were asked if we wanted to be part of the planning committee for an upcoming Valentine's Day event that would also be a fundraiser for the club.

I was so excited to be part of something with my college associates and the responsibility made me look forward to taking on similar leadership roles later in my college career. Mynoucka and I led in the plans for the event and were granted permission by the college to use the cafe facility as a night venue.

By this point, my senior year was a haze of sadness, confusion and relentless bullying by Meghan and her friends who wanted me to stop seeing Lanau. We never broke up and, in my mind, we were still a couple.

RANDOM RANT: Naturally, there is nothing Haitians love more than giving them an occasion and excuse to dress up. Like…I'm the type of chick who will show up to your pool party in a full ball gown, draped over the edges of one of those beds equipped with the four-post and four shirtless men that just happen to be carrying me into the party like I'm Mariah FUCKING Carey! 👀😋

At this point, Lanau and my relationship was barely in existence, and I struggled to understand what to believe. How he showed me he loved me or how he'd make love to me was never in alignment with his behavior or how he treated me when we were not one on one.

Lanau Ciceron was my drug and still is. It's been over 16 years and I can't even imagine a life without him in it. So yes, we stayed together even after he'd impregnated his ex-girlfriend. It's certainly not something I am proud of because I was doing it simply because I never thought I'd find a man who loved me so deeply—so passionately for just being the real me.

At the time Lanau didn't dare to tell me the truth. This is why the night of the Valentine's Day dance when he told me he'd meet me there "as my date"—I was part of the planning committee and had to be there early—I believed him.

This whole baby mama thing came without notice and caught us completely by surprise. All my friends and a few of our others who were on the planning committee—knew I was expecting to be there with him. Meghan's pregnancy was public knowledge, and everyone knew what I was not yet ready to face. Though I could see that "poor idiotic child" look in their eyes, I prayed silently that Lanau would come through for me and then maybe—just maybe, we had a real future together.

I was in denial that this baby meant that Lanau and my relationship was over. He reassured me in all our private moments that he was simply doing his fatherly duty and being there for Meghan throughout the pregnancy.

Though he told me she knew this was the case and that we were still together, there was a small part of me that knew this was likely not the case. How could I compete with a baby? Still, I wanted him to stay and be honest with everyone.

A couple of hours into the dance, Lanau showed up with his posse which included Meghan on his arm—fully dressed in black and red matching outfits, looking like the most committed-looking couple in the place.

That night, I was operating in a complete mental fog trying to understand how he could have been lying to me after all we'd been through. Watching them dance together in sync, as if no one else in the room was there, made me so sick to my stomach that I spent more than 20 minutes throwing up my insides in the bathroom, bawling uncontrollably. I had always told him to just be honest with me and until then I believed he was honoring that and never wanted to hurt me again.

They left the party together walking hand and hand—not once acknowledging me or even looking my way. I was humiliated and to mask my welling up and overflowing tears, I danced with whoever came close to me.

See, what most people don't know is that I was never permitted to date. I had many a crush but as soon as they found out who I was—or better yet, who and how my parents were when it came to anything involving the word 'dating'—let alone, 'boys', they were out just as fast as they'd arrived.

I was completely crushed and knew that whatever I thought I had with Lanau was done and over. In-person, he'd tell me that I'm the one he wanted to be with—not Meghan. And like the gullible moron that I was—I kept believing his lies over and over and over again—always mentally crossing my fingers that this time he was for real.

When Reality Shatters

Once the news of Meghan's pregnancy was completely out—we were the talk of the town (at least within our Haitian community)! Being in my senior year in high school at the time, I was laughed at in the hallways and even straight up told that I was a "stupid little bitch'' who was too "stupid" to realize Lanau was playing her for "a fool." But the truth was I was not just being an idiot—I simply could not bear to lose him. Finding Lanau helped me find myself. We accepted the raw, broken, tattered pieces of one another and realized that—we could easily fulfill all those areas we felt empty in.

After that dance, the fog of my naïve little girl lenses had been cleared. I no longer operated in fantasy and radically accepted my reality. I love Lanau in a way that physically grips my heart with all its might—making me wish for 1000 deaths over the pain of losing him in times of true anguish. A feeling my anxiety could whip up in record time at just the thought of it.

Many great American writers and beyond have analyzed the fine line between pain and love...At what cost will we trade in our dignity for just a chance at a "happily ever after?" Pure, unadulterated, wild, passionate love. I didn't have the words to explain it back then but looking back now, I know my heart always knew then what it knows now. Lanau and my love was rare. I'm grateful to the young me who had the courage to live through the dark parts.

Chapter 8 ~ Starting Us Over

"I'm not asking you to kiss me, nor apologize to me when I think you're wrong. I won't even ask you to tell me how beautiful I am—even if it's a lie, nor write me anything beautiful."

~Frida Khalo

Though my heart was breaking, I got myself together, switched on my autopilot mode, and went to school the very next day after finding out about the pregnancy. By now I was driving to school myself. As I pulled out of my high school's parking lot, I knew I could not go another moment without seeing Lanau and raced over to his house.

He was home alone and was super shocked to see me. He knew I was missing school to be there with him. As he met me in the driveway, we simply looked at one another and fell into a deep embrace.

Despite our rough start, Lanau was always the only person who could converse with me, without ever really saying a word. I missed him and I needed him at that moment. I know he needed me too. We went into his room and just cried and held each other for as long as we could.

I didn't break up with Lanau when this all went down. I know what you're thinking, why the hell not? Right? Well, to be honest, I just could not. I never had a clear moment of self-love before this man. He made me feel safe in a world where I often felt beat down and unseen—he showed me the true meaning of love, and not just love, but unconditional love.

Over the next couple of years, Lanau and I would remain in a never-ending round of limbo and though we weren't entirely together, in our hearts, we knew we were forever bound in our love. We hurt one another over and over. On our route to clarity, we eventually found our way back to each other and we never let go.

At the end of 2006, I had been diagnosed with leukemia, and Lanau and I were probably at the worst point in our relationship, when Meghan, his ex-girlfriend, and now, baby momma, had manipulated him into breaking things off with me once and for all.

This broke me in ways that I still remember to this day. After weeks of trying to track Lanau down, he finally got in touch with me on his birthday that December. I told him that I desperately needed to see him and that I also had some news. On the evening of the 28th of December in 2006, we met up in the local Toys R Us parking lot (a toy store he was working at, at the time). Formally being diagnosed the day before, I wanted nothing more than to share this news with him. But as he arrived there in his mother's white minivan, he also had a group of people with him.

He parked a way away from my car and as if an alien had taken over his body, he delivered his crushing blow first, telling me that he no longer wanted to see or be involved with me again. He told me now that he was a father, he wanted to make things work with Meghan. And just that quickly, he ran back into the van that was filled with

Meghan and her friends, and they drove away—cackling loudly at what was a planned ambush.

This was the first time I was ashamed of following my heart. I felt stupid and little. I questioned everything that had occurred between Lanau and me, up until that moment. I scolded myself for letting him in. I scolded myself for allowing myself to fall.

Still, as hard as I tried, I couldn't help but want and need my friend. I was sick and on my own. My parents were in their own world and never noticed what I was experiencing.

After weeks of ignoring me, well into the start of early 2007, I reached out to Lanau's best friend, Jude. Jude had always been a sweetheart to me and never failed to remind me that despite the life Lanau now found himself in—I was the girl he believed his friend was supposed to be with.

I wasted no time telling him about my illness in hopes that he could relay the information to Lanau. Jude was sympathetic and like the human teddy bear he was—he wished me well and said that he'd be keeping me in his prayers. He added that he knew Lanau would be reaching out if he knew what was happening.

I realize now that this was the moment I should have walked away and saved myself the heartache, but still Lanau and I found ourselves back in each other's lives. He was ashamed for walking away and breaking my heart, as I was preparing to tell him about the worst thing that could ever happen to a perfectly healthy and fit 19-year-old.

I read about Frida Khalo for the first time in the waiting room of a cold doctor's office. I was anxiously awaiting my fate at the end of multiple sterilized needles and badly needed a distraction. I picked up a random magazine on the messy pile on the table before me and opened it up to a random page. I was desperate for a thought that was not my own. Had I known at that moment that Frida's life and creative heart would have so many parallels and raw truths in common with mine, I may have slowed down and read her words a little closer. It was December 27th of 2006 and I was about to find out my life had an expiration date.

In early October of 2020, I was scrolling through Instagram and this quote with a stunning picture of Frida herself popped up and I read this quote...

"I'm not asking you to kiss me, nor apologize to me when I think you're wrong. I won't even ask you to hug me when I need it most. I don't ask you to tell me how beautiful I am, even if it's a lie, nor write me anything beautiful."

At the peaks of a ravenous depression, I met back up with my old friend and this time I only read—I listened, watched, thought and read again. In my darkest life moments, I've turned to the written word. I had no idea Frida was a metaphor for the life I've lived.

Lanau and I soon met up after I reached out to Jude. He didn't know what to say and much like I found myself when he had become a father—all he did was hold me as we sat silently in the wooden park at my old elementary school that we'd often meet at to talk and hangout.

Outside the pier at Centennial Park, downtown, this was the space we both felt drawn to and shared some of our most intimate moments.

This park was also the first place Lanau took me after I'd declared my feelings for him. We'd laugh about the fact that it was my fifth-grade class who took part in building it for the school property it sat on, Allen Park. And now here we were spending the most intimate moments of our early days of dating in the space shuttle/rocket ship that became the regular spot for our make-out sessions when neither of us was yet bold enough to "bring" or in my case—sneak a boy into my room. Oh, but Lanau was worth the trouble, and I instantly found myself not caring about being the perfect daughter my parents expected me to be.

Still, I knew his heart and the news connected us once again. I made it known that I didn't care what was happening or what anybody thought of us. I was alone and needed my best friend and the captor of my heart with me. I was willing to take him in any capacity I was allotted.

Through so many growing pains, our love for one another evolved and withstood so many trials. Six months after getting back together in March of 2008 and after officially breaking up on my birthday the year before, Lanau agreed to move to Tampa, where I was currently living and attending college at USF. Though I'm sure, his motives for moving were not entirely related to me, I think he knew this was a necessary move if we were going to allow ourselves to just be happy.

In a way, Lanau completed the raising my parents had abandoned years before when we moved in together. Lanau taught me how to be a woman, and I taught him how to be a man. By this point, we knew what we had between us was not only rare, but it was real.

For years, Lanau and I battled to keep our relationship afloat. We argued just as hard as we loved and with every encounter, we somehow never grew apart. When they say a successful relationship is two people who refuse to give up on each other, I believe that Lanau and I emulate that very concept.

When it comes down to it, I think Lanau and I were simply made to be together. We both were raised in very chaotic homes within a complicated Haitian culture, and though different, we still understood one another in a way that only soulmates could and still do.

In the summer of 2012, Lanau and I went on a mini vacation to South Beach, Miami. We were invited by our couple friends, Peyton and Merida, along with some of their friends. We jumped at the chance to go to such a beautiful place and we'd never taken part in a couples-only trip so we were eager to experience something fun and new.

Peyton had connections through his job and was able to get us into the luxurious resort, The W South Beach. This high-end hotel is THE Miami Beach spot for celebrities. We saw Shemar Moore from across the pool one day, hanging out with what seemed like a hired group of escorts, planted conveniently around him, in various colored bikinis—as if they were getting ready to film a music video in which Shemar was the rapper. We glanced over occasionally trying to play it cool amongst our friends who seemed to be pretty used to living this lifestyle.

But just as quickly as it began, as the trip went on it was not at all what we had expected. Peyton and Merida, along with their friends, often made us feel like poor losers. Being in our early 20s at the time, Lanau and I weren't exactly bankrolling so when we had to split a $300 plus dinner bill, we did our damndest to not freak out right there at the table. So we paid our part and quickly got back to our room to have the cow! Being new friends, Lanau was not quite comfortable with Peyton, who often acted like an arrogant pompous dick. His friends were all one-uppers, who crawled so far up his ass, you wondered why they didn't reek all the time!

By the second evening, Lanau and I did our best to be positive and go along just to get along for the remainder of the trip. After dinner, we went back to the hotel and all the ladies got dressed for a night on the town with our men. We met Peyton and Merida back in their suite which was huge and contained three rooms to share with the other couples. We were the only couple who were off on our own, and that worked to our advantage.

We all took lots of shots of Patron and got completely twisted. Within 20 minutes, my body was completely taken over by the liquor and I felt like partying. In the club, everything seemed louder, brighter, and very, very quick. Even though it was my first time being under this type of influence, I knew right away, I was not okay with what I was feeling and it was about to get much more intense. The night sped by, and I can't remember actively hanging out with any of the people we came with.

Nearly six in the morning, we were just catching a cab back to the hotel. Back in our private room at The W, we collapsed into the fluffy, divine white bedding and didn't move for the whole day.

I felt like shit. It wasn't like anything I'd ever experienced outside of a hangover. But patiently and affectionately, Lanau nursed me to feeling better and I spent the remainder of the trip in his arms.

Coming down from the night, Lanau and I just talked. No, we talked. Never had I seen Lanau so focused on our relationship. He was open. He was vulnerable. It was then I knew he was going to be my husband. This day led us down a path we never could have seen coming. Whether it was the effects of the drugs or simply our very awakening of what we had between us, we unleashed and lent ourselves entirely to what it was we were feeling for one another. This was also when Lanau discussed marriage with me for the first time. After that trip, we were never again the same.

By the end of the year, we once again took a chance on us and tried to have a baby. By the holidays we had conceived, and the year of 2013 started with our awareness of the family we were about to create.

When I was 14, I was at the peak of my devotion to the church and my faith. During a youth-led annual female pastor was invited to our church during a revival. If I remember correctly, she was the closing sermon for the week-long event. I was immediately enamored with her.

It was the first time I'd seen a young and female pastor preach. Up until then I'd only ever seen men delivering the sermons and leading services. It never occurred to me until that moment that a woman and a young one at that (she looked to be about mid 30s at the time) would be allowed to command a room and have the audiences' ear—respectfully.

One of my friends—can't quite remember who—but someone definitely told me that she was possibly related to Wyclef Jean, who was my musical obsession back then mostly because it was rare to find a Haitian person who was famous. Much like the rest of American world, I thought of the Haitian community as this rare sighting—considering many people's response to the fact that I was Haitian was "What's a Haitian?"

I'm almost positive it is not true that this pastor was a cousin or sister to Wyclef. At the time though it made me even more interested in what she had to say. Up until then my only true commitment was to earn my parents' love and make them proud of me—a feat that was quickly beginning to feel impossible to me.

Being a devout and fully immersed "Christian" was the gateway to their love, so I held on...and tight. I can't even remember the pastor's name anymore, though I'm sure one of the notorious, former Heavenly Stars members—aka my only true friends and surrogate family at the time—will recollect the conception of this idea.

The words that stayed with me all these years from her sermon that evening was "Success is knowing your purpose in life." She also reiterated a clever play on words—that even this wordsmith is pretty impressed by—"justif-ied"— "as in 'Just-If-I-D-idn't' have any sin. I thought about those words today and realized I have grown from and now really understand what she meant.

She was half right. Success IS knowing your purpose in life. I'm doing what I love and have built the family I always wanted for myself. But back then, my young mind took this as a definitive sign that life doesn't come with its tumbles. It does. It comes with heaps of fun, passion, love, and self-discovery—if only we're bold enough to face our authentic selves. I've come to also realize that "sin" is where our life's greatest lessons tend to come from. It's often messy, not at all easy, devastating even...

But we mustn't be afraid of sinning—for that will truly be when the true assessment of 'self' begins. I have loved, but I've never lost. Turns out you CAN 'have it all'—a lot of times it simply means you can't have all your desired successes met. This is where growth and evolution begin to truly take seed. My third eye is wide open, and I am no longer desperate or afraid of love in all its facets. For I am only evolving and clutching onto the pieces that matter most along the way. Our story is just beginning.

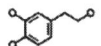

Jumping the Broom

In February of that year, we traveled down to Fort Myers from Tampa, and it was on this trip we seriously decided to get married. I was only weeks into my pregnancy with Lenoxx and so we were keeping it on the down low. We were visiting Lanau's childhood neighbor, who still lived next door to his parents.

Having watched him go from child to man, she was endearingly called Sister by Lanau and his family. She was a staple influence within Lanau's life and her opinion meant the world to him. On this visit she very bluntly questioned Lanau as to why he had not yet popped the question. Feeling uneasy, I remained quiet and left Lanau hanging as he awkwardly searched for the words to answer her. Inside I was laughing because I had been dying to have this conversation with Lanau but he always shut it down prior to this moment.

On the drive back home to Tampa, Lanau suddenly asked me what my feelings were towards getting married and how I felt about taking a plunge that year. I was silently ecstatic though I worried why he'd never decided to ask me himself—let alone, thought about it. Prior to our trip to Miami, I could never tell through our relationship whether he was serious about me in that way or just marking time to go back to being a family with Meghan and their son. It was an anxiety that stayed with me up until we were married ourselves. She was after all his first love and the one relationship that caused him the trauma he still struggles with in our marriage today.

So that was it. There was no formal proposal, no surprising Flashdance—no pomp and circumstance. To this day I always tell him—I don't care if I'm in the nursing home, ass down to my ankles, with more bags under my eyes than Kim K's closet—I want my damn proposal!

Within weeks of this conversation, we had finally broken the news to my parents who immediately went into a sudden frenzy of 'what will people think?" They urged and bullied us into getting married, and soon—for the sake of their supposed 'souls' and their roles within the clergy of their church.

Nearly in the second trimester of my pregnancy with our first child together, I felt pressured by them and I clobbered Lanau into feeling like we had to just get married and get it over with.

All we wanted to do was go to the courthouse and get married in a civil ceremony with a Justice of the Peace, but by the time my parents had dug their claws into it, it was their plans and no longer our own.

My parents' only motive for paying for the whole messy affair was simply to make it appear as though our union was not at all unexpected or unplanned. By the end, the only the vows we exchanged on the beach, in the location we chose for ourselves, bonded us—it was our non-negotiable.

Much like the weeks leading up to it, our wedding night was one for the books. Family members from both sides of our family showed up to celebrate, though it was only a few close family members. My oldest sister and her entire family attended the event. Carline was my Matron of Honor and my close college friend and former roommate, Leslie, was my maid of honor.

The day was not without its drama, but this would be the first and only times that both sides of our families were under the same roof. Though they didn't like one another, having a grandchild on the way made them willing to quail their differences for the sake of us, their kids. I was now six months along and everyone was on a mission to make me feel happy and beautiful.

RANDOM RANT: On my wedding day I did not feel beautiful. In fact, I felt like a whale in drapes and looking at myself in the mirror was rather difficult. Nothing that day looked like what Lanau and I had always imagined and it hurt to know, some of our closest friends and family members couldn't be there. We felt rushed and it became more important to maintain the peace for the baby that was soon to arrive.

The strain between our families started long before our relationship began. As a kid, I can still remember coming along with my father to various loyal customers' homes as he sold Caribbean foods, produce and other odds and ends Haitians in the states had a hard time getting their hands on.

Lanau's mom and my father's relationship, though unbeknownst to us, was rather close and trusting. In all the years we've been a couple, we've realized that our parents had relationships we were not privy to. I can only imagine that our coming together for life was never something either side of our families saw showing up on the radar.

Becoming Our Own Family

That fall, Lanau and I welcomed our baby boy, Lenoxx Kayden Ciceron, to the world. Just five pounds, 11 ounces he took our relationship to a level we never could have imagined would exist for the two of us. The love you share in creating another life together I feel is much too downplayed and not quite as immaculate as the experience truly proves to be.

I realize now that my mom and dad's only objective in pushing us into marriage had absolutely nothing to do with their desire to see me happy. I see now that I could have been pregnant with the town's local serial murderer's baby and they still would've thrown an event filled with artificial flowers just to save face before their holier-than-thou peers.

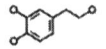

My Lanau

By now I can understand any disdain you may feel dear reader towards me or my husband. I can't defend all things, though I've personally experienced all the heartache of loving a Black man. A Black man who the world tried to proclaim unworthy or valueless. I've been blessed to see him at his best and even at his worst and, still, I am immensely blessed to have a man accept my flaws and all.

I accepted his flaws of course, but we possess a sort of love that goes beyond life's toughest moments. We're bonded together in the common traumas and shared experiences of being the children of first-generation Haitian immigrants. We both lived in the space of not fully feeling secure or safe because of the devastations that our families faced in the chaotic world that was not built for them to succeed.

Lanau—before all is my absolute best friend. He knows me inside and out and in a way that few will ever know me. We've struggled together. We've built together. We've fought together and still after all we've been through, we're still best friends at the core. As of writing this we're nearly nine years married and are looking forward to our 10th wedding anniversary when we could renew our vows in the celebration we've always dreamed of.

We always wanted a wedding with our closest friends but at the time we were marrying—in our hearts we were marrying for love but we were too young and not strong enough to not allow our families to make the decision for us.

We could barely afford a honeymoon and even though our wedding video still brings us to tears to this day. We know despite the trials and tribulations of that weekend—we married one another just as we'd always hoped and Beach Access #13 of Clearwater Beach, Florida will forever be the place where our love story was given wings and we were so blessed to have some good friends in our lives who helped us pull it off, without judgement.

To Tara and Chris Bower who helped us bring our lives together—thank you. To Marybeth, who was a chill and always genuine friend, who went out of her way to make sure we were able to have a real babymoon/honeymoon weekend. It's an honor to know you and have you in our lives.

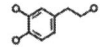

My Vows to Lanau on June 8th, 2013

So I've been going over this moment in my head repeatedly, trying to imagine the perfect words to say to you on our wedding day. Call it the perfectionist in me but I figured after almost nine years of greeting cards, just-because notes, carefully constructed playlists, and poetic with a hint of anger text messages—this was my shining moment!

This was the moment I had to pull out all the stops and really sweep you off your feet. But then it hit me—all of our most endearing moments, throughout this book we call The Adventures of Lanau and Josette, our best times were built off of imperfections and unexpected surprises.

Our relationship began and took off when we both least expected. In fact, if you had asked 16-year-old Jo and 18-year-old L, what we thought of each other, I'm pretty sure the word hate would have been thrown around quite loosely along with some other colorful additions. But overnight it would seem, I fell in love with my annoying, bullying school friend. Maybe because we both shut up for a sec and really looked into each other's eyes and saw something that perhaps had been there all along. My beautiful surprise.

With you, I learned to take off the mask I had been wearing for everyone else in my life and truly be me. A concept that was completely unfamiliar to me. I had played daughter, best friend, confidant, mother, and savior quite effortlessly but this role was my most challenging because you pushed me to be me. Through you, I found out who I really am and I wasn't afraid of her. Through you I went from a child to a woman.

One thing I've always been sure of was that no matter what direction our lives took us, whether we were together or not, you WERE my best friend and my soulmate. Polar opposites and somehow, we fit perfectly. So, as we stand here today, I can't make perfect promises to you that our lives will be magical and doused in fairy dust as history has already shown us that it's in our imperfections and unexpected moments that we grow closer to one another.

So I'll promise you this…

- *I will continue to be the woman you fell in love with everyday…*
- *I promise to continue to confusingly maneuver through unbalanced conversations about video games and characters I have never heard of… in exchange for dragging you to mind numbing chick flicks and Broadway musicals…*
- *I promise to always bring you the hot sauce and the mayo when I make you eggs and toast…even if it sounds pretty gross*
- *I promise to continue to embarrass you with my silly JoJo dance because I know it makes you smile…*
- *I promise to tell you I love you every single day as if I didn't just say it 2 mins prior…*
- *But most of all…I promise to walk this new chapter of our lives with you no matter what God throws in our ways…taking on new roles as mother to our son, teacher, dinner maker, and soccer mom (or Theater mom lol) as I play my best role yet—your wife.*

To the end and back baby, I couldn't have asked for a better partner…my beautiful surprise.

Chapter 9 ~ She Never Said a Word

"A little while ago—not much more than a few days ago, I was a child who went about in a world of colors. My friends, my companions, became women slowly; I became old in instants."

~Frida Khalo

DECEPTION

She never said a word

Still, there was plenty to be said.

Her emerald guards shielded all harm and the fetus lay cradled at her feet.

Relax, unwind, you're safe with me...caroled her inviting flames.

Consoling, forgiving, she'll always be—no sanctuary, no place, I could ever truly seek.

From beginning to end she was a sister, the mother—an old, dear friend.

No greater spell or menacing destruction could bring about such a separating rift.

*But she saw it **all** and heard it **all**.*

Her once praised loyalty soon became my damning defeat.

*She **saw** it that day and all the days after.*

*The pain and agony; she could have said what she had witnessed in these... **in these, her ensnaring walls**.*

But loyal she remained, not once did she ever speak or explain the horrors she seen that early afternoon.

*And my mind could not forgive her for what I could not bring **myself to say**.*

It had taken place within this cell, once a fortress of solitude, now a fortress of scarlet hell. When they came and they saw, they ripped her sheets and pulled at her teeth.

They knew but I could not say and I looked at my friend and she looked away.

No longer my night and shining armor;

Her emerald guards now possessed an unappealing power,

Once twenty feet tall—now six feet deep.

They poked and prodded me, interrogating with their beams of doubt,

But I remained muted—and my friend did too.

Though I silently prayed she wasn't going to...she had not.

Perhaps she was unaware that I called for her to reveal his malevolent snare.

*"Tell them please!" I begged in my head, for I could never find the courage in me—to **free** myself.*

Ransacked in horror, altered in fear, once a comforting hold—

Now stood so dreary and cold.

She was no longer my companion, to whom I once told every secret and every dream.

She was now, a mirage of my past, a reminder of what I lacked.

Her walls, now a video screen replaying those sinful moments when he beat, soiled, and battered me with no restrains, no boundaries, and no care…

For she had no say, in what she could no longer repair.

Her mocking ceiling caved in at dark, taunting me with its withering stares and eyes that never shut.

*And our friendship had ended that last day when she decided to be **just a room**—and that is how she stayed.*

This is a poem I wrote as a very angry teenager, who had very little self-esteem, and who desperately sought the validation and approval of others. As children, we're conditioned to believe that adults know everything and are always right. In the Haitian culture we are taught to always be submissive to someone older than us—though it seems like most parents, never quite understood the danger that came with that messaging that immediately disarmed a child victim who found themselves in a dangerous situation.

For most of my life, I've agonized over the dark memories I had throughout my upbringing at the hands of adults who my parents trusted. There's a disturbing pattern of this sort of devious behavior amongst many cultures but as Haitian American, it's a tale I've heard too often from most Haitian girls I grew up with.

I was sexually assaulted at various times throughout my childhood by older men and even boys in my teen years. I never felt safe enough nor was I ever given the space to speak openly about it. Having two older sisters who went through so much before me, I learned pretty quickly that the topic of sex was never to be spoken of in any way, shape, or form which honestly silenced me.

Religion played a major factor into my fears of speaking up because the messaging I always got was that I was going to hell if I even thought about it. After a while, I began to think that these things happened to me because something was wrong with me. By the time I was 15, I settled on the thought that it was my fault and that somewhere along the line, I'd done something so bad that I deserved to be hurt.

For years I even tried to pretend it was all a bad dream and the older I got, the harder those traumas became to ignore. When I began seeing a therapist so much was flooded in my thoughts. That combined with the new hardships of being in a place like Alexandria, I began feeling hopeless. I couldn't recognize myself and was mentally battling the terrified little girl that still lived inside me.

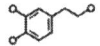

Scarlet Letter

Many of the messages—and my inability to access adults who I felt would listen and believe me—scared me into submission whenever I was exposed to something or someone who was incredibly inappropriate with me, a little girl. I did what any man told me to do because I was scared to tell anyone how many times, between the ages of five and seventeen, I was placed in vulnerable and dangerous situations I couldn't speak up about. For the longest time I remained angry at my five-year-old self. I believed I was actually cursed and attracted predatory energy.

As my body began developing early, Haitian and Black boys would often equate my body type to my virtue. I spent a lifetime trying to scrub off that scarlet letter. But deep down I genuinely believed that this was why boys only sought to hurt me and never chose me for me.

Being called a "slut" when you'd never been with anyone throughout high school further destroyed my self-perspective. Once Lanau came into the picture and Baby Gate happened. The rumors people around us created about me now being "easy"—gutted my confidence.

For a couple of years until I moved out of Fort Myers in 2008, I got made fun of by girls for being foolish enough to date someone who would be with a girl with Meghan's reputation. She was the Haitian Jezebel and this somehow equated to shitty guys in our community believing they too had a shot at me.

Nonetheless, the bullying was really hurtful and made me very focused on getting the heck out of dodge. Amid all these issues, my health still remained a concern and I literally took my life into my own hands and made decisions medically for myself. I'm choosing to not go into the details of my illness because it is still an area in my life, I'm still working on processing and forgiving those who were supposed to love me through it all.

I never processed all the things that happened to me. I just thought the answer was to make my parents love me more. My trauma temporarily repressed itself as my relationship changed and matured with Lanau. While I certainly don't make excuses for the pain he's caused me in the past, I retreated and always found a reason to keep taking the hurt—just like I had been conditioned to do with men. I could have run into many more monsters but the universe brought me Lanau instead. That's a situation people don't have to understand, so long as we do.

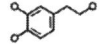

After we got married I felt protected and imagined the curse had been lifted. In 2018, we went on vacation to Jamaica. It was our fifth wedding anniversary and we'd worked really hard to make this trip happen. In a random run-in with a hotel employee, I thought that I was being led to the women's restroom I couldn't find on my own.

Out of nowhere, I found myself being pulled into a dark maintenance room with this stranger who stood at about 6'4, pushing up against my 4'10 body. Horrified I was about to be raped as he kept trying to bend me over. Crying, all I could think at the moment was to distract him and keep him calm.

I began flirting and negotiating with him to let me go. When he began holding me down, I pushed up with all my might and started doing oral on him. It seemed to be working and he wasn't trying to control my body.

As some footsteps approached the door, I could see he was nervous about being heard as he began shushing me. Taking a risk, I began to speak up louder telling him to let me go or I was going to scream. He could've easily knocked me out and had his way but I just couldn't be someone's victim anymore. I fought this time and I did what I had to do, to come out alive.

I managed to get away and immediately went looking for my husband to let him know what had happened. Angry and sad I even had to experience this, I made sure we filed a report with the resort and had the employee fired.

This triggered back all those memories I'd been repressing from my childhood and for a second in that maintenance room, I was that five-year-old little girl again who'd just picked a spot on the wall to stare at and wait for it to be over. Therapy is what gave me the will to fight past my traumas at that moment and I *needed* to come home to my babies.

For months after that trip, Lanau spent endless nights waking up with me and holding me as I had recurring nightmares about every traumatic sexual experience I'd had throughout my life. He struggled himself mentally feeling he had failed to protect me on our trip, though I continued to assure him there was no way we could've seen that coming. He continued to remind me how much stronger I was than thought of myself. He reminded me that I was safe and slowly but surely the nightmares subsided.

To all my fellow Haitian peeps women *and* men—let's break this cycle now. Let's end this trauma cycle and the need to be silent about things that may bring shame to our families. That shit is rooted so deeply that you could go your entire life suffering from things they failed to protect you from.

I believe in the power of conversations, and I know this one we've been sweeping under the rug for far too long. I'm healing so my daughter won't have to do it for me as I pass it on to her. Generational trauma has seeped into so much of who we are as a culture that our babies quite literally can't afford, *nor* do they deserve such a fate.

I decided to intentionally keep myself from being part of someone else's trauma by leading with empathy, love, and understanding in all that I do. I'm still on my healing path and still have many more stones to turn over—and for once in my life, I *know* I *am* going to be okay.

Chapter 10 ~ My Dark Passenger

"I tried to drown my sorrows but the bastards learned how to swim."

~Frida Kahlo

I was officially diagnosed with general anxiety, PTSD, and depression back in 2016. I think on some level I've always been aware that something was especially different with me. I learned early on that my thinking was not in alliance with the social norm. I always fixated on things that drove my parents crazy so once again, I kept those things to myself.

I remember the day I came across the word "worrywart" in a book I was reading. I was about 8 and remember thinking, "That's me…" I worried about everything—what people thought about me, what my parents thought about me. I worried about my schoolwork and never wanted to look stupid. I always thought about the absolute worst-case scenario of everything and was pretty convinced these ideas were real and would happen.

My best friend Mynoucka was a really fast reader and in my mind, because I wasn't reading quite at the same pace, that meant I wasn't a good reader. I LOVED reading but found myself keeping the books I was indulging in, as I got older—to myself so I wouldn't feel pressured to read something quickly. I enjoyed taking my time, reading great parts over and over again dreaming of the day I could be a writer, putting out incredible stories.

Today, I know that my friends really wouldn't care whether I was a fast reader. But here's the tricky thing about negative self-talk and anxiety—if you hear those thoughts in your head enough times it only grows in its strength, according entirely to you. I kept this "I'm not a good reader" mindset throughout my schooling and even into my college years. Insecurity popped up in my mind when I was just a child and it remained in my subconscious and made me feel awful about myself.

When we'd take tests in school that were timed—just hearing the students around me flip pages before me or get up before me to turn in their completed exams, made me panic. I worried about looking like I was the slow or stupid one. This test anxiety lasted throughout my college years which demolished any confidence I had in what I could do. When people would call me smart—I felt like a fraud and usually just smiled awkwardly—convinced they were secretly seeing through my sham.

I know now that this was my "Dark Passenger" hovering nearby my whole life. Yes, I swiped that concept from the popular crime drama television series that aired on Showtime from 2006 to 2013, Dexter. Though Dexter's "Dark Passenger" was the insatiable need to kill people—my Dark Passenger is the vessel that houses my mental demons: anxiety, depression, and PTSD. My Dark Passenger has an insatiable need to destroy me mentally and obliterate my self-esteem.

I can relate to this concept not only because let's face it—I loved the show and labeling my mental health as my Dark Passenger made me feel less like a victim of my negative thoughts and more like a badass woman who's well-aware of her flaws and doesn't allow them to define her.

Random Rant: I have a love/hate relationship with my anxiety. My anxiety makes me extremely self-aware because I'm always fixated on what's going to happen next. At the same time however, my anxiety keeps me from staying and remaining in the moments. If I had to say what the worst part of it all is, it's knowing that you're missing so much of the world around you. You're bonded to your thoughts at all times. Logan Huntzberger from *Gilmore Girls* put it best when he was pushing Rory to step out of her comfort zone, "People can live 100 years without really living for one minute."

Once we moved to Minnesota 2015, those first couple years, I was so depressed and lonely—I questioned everything I thought I knew about myself. Though academics didn't feel like my strong suit despite having always been a good student—I knew my true talents were in my writing.

I loved writing about people, real-life and just studying the minds, lives, and teachings of figures like Malcolm X, Maya Angelou, and of course—Frida Kahlo. As a child I'd read books like *Little Women*, *Pride and Prejudice*, *Huckleberry Finn*, and *Are You There God? It's Me, Margaret*.

I was addicted to these writings and the complexity of these character's lives. I now know that I read these vastly different genres because I was looking for myself within them. These characters made me feel like it was okay to be different and not fit in.

I was officially diagnosed with anxiety in the summer of 2016, after seeking help for what was far more than the Mommy Blues. I was a new mom of two, in a new town, in a new state, with no family or friends. I was utterly alone which was rather ironic because I wasn't alone. At least, not in the physical sense. I had my amazing husband, my quirky son, and a vibrant baby girl who amazed me by simply existing.

While postpartum very much played a role in my anxiety at the time, it was accelerated by the extremities of my recent leap of faith, when we literally started over, moving to Alexandria from Florida, less than a year before my diagnosis.

Spending 10 to 12 hours a day alone while Lanau worked became overwhelming, to say the least. No matter how organized I was or how focused I tried to be, I found myself backed into a dark space in my mind. I didn't feel worthy of my husband or my kids. I felt like I was letting them down. I thought they were better off without me. I was afraid of my own thoughts.

Throughout my periods of isolation after the move to Minnesota—I began confronting these insecurities and found that having grown up and matured into a pensive and deeply analytical young woman. I realized many of the things that I found difficult to comprehend when I was younger was clouded by the pressure of getting a passing grade, balancing other classes and keeping up with my friends. My parents only cared about that 'A' or 'B' on my report card at the end of that quarter or semester.

I was too embarrassed to tell my teachers and professors the truth about my testing anxiety. I always did well on written exams but would be completely frazzled if a multiple-choice test was coming up. My anxiety was so bad I would stay up all night reading the chapters and testing material over and over again, scared that I'd forget everything if I slept.

What I found when I revisited all these concepts at 29, 30, and 31was that I not only comprehended these things but I loved being able to revisit these ideas and having lived enough life—I was never stupid or slow. I was just a kid who wasn't given positive affirmations by the adults in her life and needed a different method of testing than others. My fear of failure crippled my ability to just be confident that I, like everyone else, could be great and do great things.

My Dark Passenger keeps me in a constant cycle of fear. Fear of failing. Fear of amounting to nothing. Fear of ending up alone. Fear of losing people. When you spend your entire life being reminded by the people you love that their love is not at all unconditional—but can very easily be taken away if I was no longer of use to them.

This showed up in my incessant need as a little girl to gain my parents' approval and hear how proud of me they were. My dad didn't take so much work because just like the Virgo tendencies we both shared, I did my best to please him and stole a hug and "I love you" whenever I had a chance. My mother on the other hand was a tough sell. She wasn't particularly affectionate and seemed incredibly uncomfortable with words or even acts of affection.

You can always count on her to tell you when you've done something wrong or how you could've done better. I still wonder if this was just something she wasn't aware she does or if it was purposeful to make me humble or perhaps that there was always room for improvement.

In general, mental health is just not acknowledged in our Haitian culture. Speaking about your feelings was not only weak but it gave others ammunition to label you as "crazy" or "unstable." My mom seemed to also have her anxieties about how our family was portrayed in public amongst our Haitian peers. She wanted us to always appear clean, together, and well-dressed. She expected us to be well-spoken, very polite, and most importantly to only offer opinions when asked. She would take it as a personal assault if we dared to speak out of turn within the presence of other Haitian adults and you could almost guarantee a backhanded slap was forthcoming if you were daring or stupid enough to say something that was meant to remain a secret.

My Dark Passenger remains in the back of my thoughts, fearing me into submission at any chance She gets. After years of therapy, I now know that She represents my fears. My anxiety feeds me lies that I actively try to navigate every single day.

Sometimes the lies are about my mothering abilities, my worthiness as a wife and partner, or my overwhelming fear of never having the career I truly desire. Other times, I'm immersed in irrational worries of our politically chaotic, divided and increasingly hateful world.

If my husband is late coming home from work, my chest begins to tighten at the thought of him being in an accident or worse, being pulled over by a cop. At the height of these fears, if left uninterrupted, my mind will spin into an anxiety attack, often leaving me in the fetal position, gasping for air.

The ADAA defines anxiety attacks as the abrupt onset of intense fear or discomfort that reaches a peak within minutes. Palpitations, pounding heart, or an accelerated heart rate are all symptoms that are often linked with anxiety attacks.

My anxiety attacks are generally at the height of highly stressful situations that even if they may seem menial on the outside, they're wildly exaggerated in my mind, leading me down the rabbit hole of believing I am, in all sincerity, on the brink of death. No matter how illogical the thought may be, in that moment the only voice I can hear is Hers.

In light of such anxieties, people tend to search their memory for a similar instance when they first remember feeling this way. For many people, including myself, anxiety is attached to a traumatic childhood experience. Coming from an abusive home, I experienced trauma on a myriad of occasions that has left me feeling broken.

This year, I was raised out of the proverbial "Sunken Place" by claiming my power back over my mind. For the longest time, I believed my anxiety was a weakness. I would beat myself up for being unable to escape such terrorizing thoughts and feelings.

One day, a particularly intense therapy session, I came to realize just how much I had overcome throughout my life. From an abusive childhood to surviving Leukemia at 19-years-old to defying all odds in not just one high-risk pregnancy—two high-risk pregnancies!

Suddenly, I realized how wrong I was. My anxiety has been a driving force propelling me through some of my greatest life battles. Therapy helps me to resolve that internal conflict and be truly comfortable in my own skin, without the mask. Clinically, psychologists refer to this as integration.

Working towards integration has helped me regain control of my thoughts, subsiding my anxiety. Admittedly, I'm not quite there yet. I still have a long way to go in my journey. Only now, I am hopeful and feel empowered to claim mental freedom.

Part of my therapist's teachings have been to intentionally carve out times to just sit alone with my thoughts. I try to find moments throughout my day to simply disconnect from the world. Though this is challenging with a five-year-old and two-year-old, even if it's a few minutes after the kids have gone to bed or early in the morning before they wake up. I make it a priority to give myself time to reflect and be still.

Today, my Dark Passenger is a regular part of my life and after nearly four years of therapy, I'm learning to accept the things that make me different but not at all broken. By the time I started seeing my therapist after giving birth to my daughter—I remembered all the things I've endured at the hands of parents who never healed from their own childhood traumas.

 My dad lost his mother at just eight-years-old and overnight became the man of the house when my grandfather no longer was mentally capable of taking care of his three children. My father was now responsible for his family's survival and knew at eight-years-old his life would never again be the same. My grandfather was a violent drunk who often made my father his sole focus to beat on whenever he failed to earn enough money doing work around the village. Everyone knew the life this little boy was now living.

After losing her father, my mother, her 11 siblings, and now, single mom had to find a way to keep going. Having daughters, my mom was essentially sold into an arranged courtship with a man who was a cruel sexual deviant. She was angry. She didn't speak to most of her family for well over 20 years and was suddenly living in a country of which she felt on the outside culturally.

Generational trauma is so real in my culture and in all communities of color. If you never heal from your wounds, you are sure to bleed on people who never cut you. Much like poverty, unacknowledged trauma rolls right onto our children's shoulders.

Trauma is what kept me silent whenever I found myself in an abusive situation with older men who knew they were preying on a little girl. This pattern of trauma also kept me from living a full life that wasn't riddled with anxiety, depression, and PTSD.

The gift therapy gave me in my 30s was a level of clarity and self-awareness I didn't know I was missing. 2020 was the year I realized what all that therapy had done for me. Between the daily news jam-packed with stories of people dying from the COVID-19 pandemic, to Black and Brown men and women being murdered by the police—the realities of my life and the world around me began melding together.

A letter I wrote to the editor of the local town paper *Echo Press*:

Okay, Alexandria. Let's Talk About It…

As a Black woman who has lived with my share of discrimination and straight up racism in Alexandria over the last five years, I could not sit back and watch this type of ignorant, uneducated, utterly hurtful and dangerous rhetoric to continue to spread around the community where myself and many BLACK families, along with other families of color work, live, and raise our families. I must speak up for my community and our REAL LIVED experiences that this town seems to be so keen on dismissing—if it's acknowledged at all.

But first, some background: What is "Black Lives Matter?"

Black Lives Matter is a MOVEMENT. It was a direct response to the murder of 17-year-old Trayvon Martin, who's case in 2013 ended with a complete acquittal of his killer, George Zimmerman who thought he looked "suspicious" while walking home, armed with a hoodie, pop and a pack Skittles!

#BlackLivesMatter began as a call to action in response to all the state-sanctioned violence, racial profiling, and brutality (i.e., systemic racism) that has been taking place for far too long. The intention is to connect Black people all over the world, with a shared desire for justice.

What Are They Trying to Accomplish?
End the war on Black and Brown people.

Reparations for past and continuing harms. (Did you know Black people have spent more years in bondage than they have free? Facts! 1619 through 1865 is a total of 246 years of enslavement. We've only been "free" for 155 years!)

Divestment from institutions that criminalize, cage and harm our people.

Re-Invest in the education, health and safety of our communities.

Economic justice for ALL and reconstruction of the economy to ensure our communities have collective OWNERSHIP and not merely access.

Community control of laws, institutions and policies that most impact us.

Independent Black political power and Black self-determination in all areas of society.

Now, Let's Talk About This "I Don't See Color" Thing...

It sounds pretty, only it doesn't mean what you think it does. To "not see color" is to dismiss the existence of an entire race of people along with their centuries of pain, oppression, and generational trauma. More specifically:

It allows you to ignore racial issues because they don't directly impact you or your loved ones.

You can't fix something you can't see!

You aren't actively dismantling and addressing your own implicit biases—AND WE ALL HAVE THEM.

It limits your ability to appreciate individualism and cultures outside of your own.

Aside from the fact that "Black Lives Matter" is a TRUE statement, we must stop ignoring the history that led us here in the first place. This movement is a cry for help from a community who is just TIRED. Tired of begging. Tired of pleading. Tired of losing. Tired of dying. Tired of hashtagging—and STILL, it's not enough to convince you that we're drowning in oppression! We KNOW all lives matter! We just NEED YOU TO SEE THE PAIN AND SUFFERING THAT IS HAPPENING AROUND OUR MEN, WOMEN, and EVEN CHILDREN.

NO, our community is not perfect. We're just asking for a chance to raise our families in the same privileged world yours are without the dark cloud of racism hanging over their heads. No matter how accomplished, educated, or successful we are—there's nothing we can do to make our skin less "threatening." All lives cannot matter if Black lives DON'T matter!

While we're on the subject, please stop saying…

"Blacks"—Instead say "Black people." We're not things or a problem you need to exterminate.

"I have Black friends!"—Especially when you're about to use them as a token to justify racist views.

"I experienced racism one time…"—BLACK PEOPLE LIVE WITH RACISM AND MICROAGGRESSIONS EVERY. SINGLE. DAY—especially here in Alexandria. Do not presume to know or deny the validity of their experiences.

Countering police brutality arguments with "What about Black-on-Black Crime?"—NO CRIME IS THE RESULT OF BLACKNESS OR WHITENESS! Crime is crime.

To my fellow Black and Brown brothers and sisters in Alexandria—I see you. I feel you. I LOVE and honor you. You are NOT alone. Take heart. Keep going and look for the do-ers—we ARE here!

Sincerely,

A Tired Black Woman

~Jo Ciceron with the support of fellow POC, Preeti Yonjon Feist and The Inclusion Network

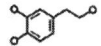

By September 2020, I was falling deeper and deeper into a depression. Everything felt hopeless and I felt completely overwhelmed with my daily life of parenting special needs kids, producing and hosting the talk show, working from home, doing the podcast, and being a wife. I was losing hope in what I was fighting for as I heard the outcomes of Breonna Taylor's murder and watched how case by case our society continued to dismiss the pain and oppression Black communities. I was failing in all areas and began thinking the people in my life would be better off without me.

The thoughts of suicide stopped being just thoughts, and now started becoming fantasies and even planning. My Dark Passenger made me believe I was a waste of a life. I was ashamed of the depths of my mental health and couldn't imagine myself ever being happy. Though Lanau had been by side through it all—he knew something about *this* moment of despair was different.

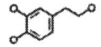

The Undoing

As tears pool, burning through my squeezed shut eyes,

I eased the triple blades over my inner thigh, pushing the razor firmly into my skin pulling in the opposite direction until I felt the release of breaking skin.

Though my heart still throbbed with pain, this little nick now puddling blood beneath me on the cold bathroom floor gave me a sense of relief and control in a moment when nothing felt like it could ever be right again.

So I did it again and again—and again.

~Jo Ciceron

In late October 2020, I attempted to take my own life twice in less than 12 hours. In my head, I had already made my peace with what I felt I needed to do to free the family of my traumas and my torturing, ongoing melancholia. The thing about mental illness is that you're not operating in reality at all BUT you seem to be the only one who's unaware of what's happening to you.

Lost in a fog of depression, I begged my husband to let me go and to let me do it. I grabbed all my prescriptions and frantically fumbled to swallow all of them before Lanau could get to me. Unsuccessful in taking any before he found me, I fought with him as I pleaded with him with reasons and justifications as to why this made sense. He carried me into our bed and held me tightly as we bawled together over what was happening.

He just kept saying, "Baby, I need you—we need you." He knew this wasn't me and I knew I was hurting him talking like this. The next morning, I cried silently next to him, completely devastated I was still alive and my Dark Passenger remained alongside me.

For a week, Lanau hid my meds and would administer them to me himself. I could see the pain and hurt in his eyes having to micromanage me that week and I was heartbroken I had put him through that. It took me several days to pull myself out of the constant suicidal-thoughts mode. Every time it crept back into my mind, I remembered what I have put Lanau through and imagined what he and the kids could've been dealing with had I been successful.

I could've easily kept this story to myself, but I wanted you to know that mental health is an ongoing process. I survived my attempt because my husband held on to me even when he didn't understand what I was feeling. My Dark Passenger is a part of me but she's certainly not ALL of me. In my quest to be unapologetic, I'm committing to being so, even when it doesn't make me feel strong to say out loud. I just want you dear reader to understand—there's no honor or pride in suffering silently. You're enough and you deserve to not just survive but live.

For an overly anxious mind such as mine, this has played a key role in learning to live with my anxiety. It's also given me room to grow in my confidence as an individual, a wife, a mother, and a writer/creator.

Changing my perspective through therapy, continual faith and prayer, I am proud to refer to my anxiety now, as my greatest superpower. My anxiety is driven by irrational fears which leaves me with only two options: Forget Everything And Run *or* Face Everything And Rise. I've chosen the latter.

So, dear reader, whom I know can certainly relate. You are not alone. You are strong. You are loved. You are powerful enough to silence the voices in exchange for the only one that truly matters—your own.

Beautifully Complicated

Every day I walk over to the drawer that houses all the many drugs that I must take daily to maintain my health. Some aid in my physical care but most are there to protect me from myself and my Dark Passenger. I sigh deeply and I give myself my daily pep talk about the importance of being the very best version of me for my family. Take a breath and just swallow.

You think I'd be used to it but I'm not. I can still remember the first prescription I was told I'd have to take in order to manage my migraines. I was 12 years old and deeply confused by all this puberty stuff that was happening to my body that I could no longer control. I had no idea it would be the start of a toxic relationship I'd be bound to for most of my life.

I have a therapist. I'm taking the drugs and doing the work but I'd be lying if I said I didn't have days I wished this was not how my body worked and even worse—are the days I hate myself for being this way in the first place. Depression, anxiety and PTSD have occupied space and taken up residence in my life. They make up a lot of what makes me, me.

Naturally uninvited, I carry the torch every day of just keepin' on, keepin'on-ing. The storms are rough and consume every part of me when I'm not on track. So I will try. I struggle but I continue to show up for my husband and my babies because they're the physical reminders that my life matters to someone.

I'm not ashamed to admit the current wave has proven stronger than those that have come before it. Yet here I stand, unmoving and enduring. There's no right or wrong way, or even destination for mental health. One must simply and yet, not so simply, learn to tighten the grip when everything is screaming at you to let go.

If you or someone you love struggle with mental illness, give them grace, give them space. Most importantly give them love because they're already struggling with loving who they are. Please do not judge what you do not personally experience.

Chapter 11 ~ Family Matters

There isn't enough time there, isn't enough nothing. There is only reality. What once was is long gone! What remains are the transparent roots appearing transformed into an eternal fruit tree. Your fruits already give scent your flowers give color blooming in the joy of wind and flower."

~Frida Khalo

My family hasn't been—well, "a family" since I got married in 2013. Asmite and her husband were not on speaking terms with my parents over a silly church issue and things remain the same. When I was about 17 going on 18 the church my sisters and I grew up in fell apart over some scandal that had the entire congregation divided into three new churches that didn't see eye to eye on the major issues that were taking place in the church.

When this happened, I lost faith in the church and church-going individuals. In a way, it was liberating. I was old enough to fill my days with work at my part-time job at HomeGoods. This allowed me to have a new excuse for not having to be at any church on Sunday on account that that was a day I was now "required" to work. Aside from school, work is the last thing a Haitian parent will say no to. The more financially independent we were—the less we kids were dependent on them for funds.

My family was never close, and I had a relationship with

my two oldest sisters that often made me feel like I was just a nuisance to them as a child. My sister Carline and I are only four years apart, and though there were lots of fighting moments between us we shared as children, Carline was my very first best friend. We both lived this sheltered life and were each other's confidante and best playmate for a while.

As Carline blossomed into her teen years, our relationship quickly changed from a playmate to us barely speaking to one another outside of bickering matches we had over pretty much everything. Carline was angry and she had good reason to be. She was a bit overweight which my parents never missed an opportunity to remind her that she "if she could just lose the weight" then... Their concern wasn't over her well-being but rather the side-eyes and stares they were receiving from our very opinionated and blunt Haitian community members.

My sister and I look a lot alike and I always considered her to be the "pretty" sister. I admired how motivated she was to be the best at everything. She was super creative and a talented artist. My parents didn't buy us toys or cool games that were in and so before she became too cool to hang out with her baby sister anymore—she would create our own board games like checkers so we could play together.

When she started middle school, she was involved in all of these activities like dance and orchestra. She drew just about as much as she breathed, and I always wanted to find my talent as she did. By 15, Carline was no longer going to put up with name-calling, whispers, rumors, or humiliation. I can still recall the day my mother made an embarrassing testimony at a church gathering that was taking place at my friend's home.

At the end of these services, people would stand up, one by

one, and deliver what we Haitian Baptists called a testimony. These were the moments people would take the opportunity to ask for prayer on a particular hardship or setback they or their loved ones were experiencing. People would ask for prayers for sick relatives in the hospital, a husband looking for a new job, or even someone who was on the verge of losing their home or worse—being deported back to Haiti.

After a couple of people had delivered their testimonies, my mother took to the floor and began asking for service members to help her pray for her family and in particular, her daughter, Carline who was struggling to lose weight and was being taunted by kids her age and even Haitian adults.

By now you know that image and reputation in the Haitian culture is everything. It wasn't so much about being genuine, good, and giving people—it was more about appearing to be the most devout, the most successful, and the one who had it all together. My mom had been hearing the rumblings about Carline and her weight throughout the community, and instead of addressing it within the privacy of our home, she felt it was best to host a PSA in the middle of a stranger's home and mortify my sister in the cruelest way I thought possible. I could not understand why a mother would do such an awful thing.

Carline was in tears the entire way home and just seeing the hurt in her eyes, I felt shattered for her and whispered, "I'm so sorry." This moment was traumatizing to my sister, and she never forgave the embarrassment she was dished out by our mom.

Asmite was born and raised by our grandmother in Haiti until she came to live with us in Florida when she was 14 years old. She was one of the most beautiful girls I'd ever seen. And though we were instructed to call her sister, my parents never actually informed Carline and me of her existence until the day she walked into our first Florida apartment before moving into our childhood home. They casually told us she was our sister and would be living with us from now on.

For days I stared at her like a little creep—just fascinated with how beautiful she was and couldn't understand how she could be my sister when she looked nothing like Carline or me. I didn't understand this as a kid but my father legally adopted Asmite as his once he had established himself in the country and made sure our little family had everything we needed to be secure.

Asmite was and is just a bright and happy spirit. Never really shy, she loved to make me laugh and I'd watch in amazement whenever she did her hair or makeup. She looked just like the girls dressed in the 90's hit TV show, *Saved By the Bell*.

Because she was older, she was given more privileges than Carline and me. Seeing her get accustomed to living in an American world intrigued me. I wanted to wear what she wore, watch what she watched and just be as beautiful as she was. Asmite was nothing like our family and differed so much from my mother, it was hard processing the fact that she was my mother's child from another relationship.

We grew closer as I got older as Asmite has always had a carpe diem way of living and just wanted to live life, have fun, and do great things. We were a lot alike and often bonded over my parent's overbearing ways and expectations that you never grow up, be human, or want to develop a social life and romantic relationships. For a while in my early 20s she was the only person in my family who understood my need to keep all things about me to myself in order to keep my mother's toxic, old-school, patriarchy-draped beliefs and unsolicited opinions out of my personal relationships.

My mother, however, saw Asmite as a personal project and an attempt to undo the wrong she believed she'd done in leaving her in Haiti with my grandmother in order to escape the relationship with Asmite's biological father. It was clear she felt guilty for doing so but out loud, she always found a way to justify her choices with the fact that we were kids who grew up in a developed, law and order country in comparison to her tough 1950's, third-world country upbringing.

Their relationship was tense, and my mother seemed to have a very personal affront to my sister's entire being and the whole way in which she was brought into this world. I struggle to think of a positive memory in which they got along genuinely and shared a light moment. I'd be lying if I could remember any light moments between us three girls and our mom. She was clearly still angry and had unresolved issues with Asmite's dad but refused to speak a good word about him—that is, when she chose to speak of those days or him at all.

Whenever my mother got into arguments with my sister—she'd throw her father's evil ways in her face as if Asmite had some control over how she was conceived. But my mother is certainly not known for making the most sense or having the most stable or popular outlook on life.

Most people in my family's life knew that my mother was

not to be messed with and much like us, could not comprehend why she appeared to always be angry or have a nasty attitude whenever anyone outside of our family was around. For most of my life I would go on and still wonder who she really is, and why did it always feel like she found it burdening to be pleasant, friendly, and approachable.

Asmite and my mother's relationship has remained broken and seemingly, permanently. When she was about 17, Asmite got tired of being my mother's emotional and oftentimes physical punching bag and went looking for her biological dad. My mom was never emotionally available, and Asmite spent her entire teenage years trying to be the daughter she wanted. But it always felt like my mother wanted nothing short of absolute perfection from her in all areas of life.

She grew lonely living in a new world with a mother who constantly reminded her that she never "wanted" her in the first place, and a stepdad who was only willing to do whatever it took to keep the peace in his marriage. Going from cousin to cousin, she eventually tracked her father's contact information down and would often walk to the nearby Publix grocery store to call him on the once everywhere, pay-phones.

I seemed to be the sister she trusted most and every now and then I'd tag along on one of her infamous phone dates with her biological dad. She seemed comforted by his friendliness and very different and friendly personality—so unlike our mom. I loved watching her smile when she spoke to him, and she'd always give me quarters to run into the store to buy a bag of chips. After all, I seemed to be the only one who saw and heard her silently crying in her bedroom at night after an all-too-often argument with our mother.

Much like she did with all of us, she always treated Asmite like she was not only an airhead, but also a whore who was obviously sleeping around since she liked wearing cute short skirts and attending high school events and games like a normal teen.

I often wondered what it was she saw in my sister that she loathed so much. Did she see herself and was just projecting and acting out? In many ways she was this super serious and mature woman and in other ways I could see this hurt child who's never been taught it's okay to just be human and lead with love over animosity.

Asmite and I had similar relationships with my mother. I still struggle to understand why we couldn't have a relationship where we not only heard and listened to each other, but one in which we actually knew one another. The older I got it became easier to shut them out than to constantly take in their criticism, disapproval, and controlling ways.

Today my mom and I are civil—at least as civil as a bitter Haitian mom could be and she still struggles to respect my boundaries. I always dreamed of having a positive Lorelai and Rory Gilmore type of mother-daughter relationship with her. But we are far from it. Because we rarely speak beyond the surface shit, "Hi. How are you doing? How are the kids?"

2019 was the first wedding anniversary my parents actually called Lanau and I to say, "Happy Anniversary" and actually acknowledged my husband's existence. It was also the first time they wanted to speak to him since that fateful night in my childhood home that started with a prayer and a life without my parents.

I was afraid to tell them when I was pregnant with Katarina in late 2015 into early 2016. I was six months along before I told them. Instead of congratulating me, they offered condolences as if this was just another mistake they felt I was making. Though I had gone through hell and back to have my two babies—I found myself telling them I was for sure going to get my tubes tied in hopes of gaining a little bit of their approval, respect and appease them.

When it came time to follow through with it—I convinced myself I was making a smart decision based on my health and past miscarriages and high-risk pregnancies. But honestly—I just wanted to stop being the loser daughter they told their church-friends about in order to shame me and having people feel sorry for their not having a relationship with me or my children.

After Katarina's birth, I thought for sure regardless of their disappointment in my life choices, I thought my parents, especially my mom, would still honor the Haitian traditions of the mother always spending the first few weeks staying with their daughter after she has delivered a baby.

But not even that moved them to be human and simply meet me where I was at in my life. I desperately needed them, and I couldn't tell them that. They sent stuff for the baby and for me to take care of myself as she would've had she made the trip to visit me in Minnesota. Still, I waited for the fateful call, and it never came.

Two months after delivering Rina, I had a tubal ligation. I wouldn't have any more kids. Since my parents didn't feel I was financially stable enough to have more children, they wouldn't need to be ashamed of me. That was crushing and was the tipping scale of my growing postpartum depression. At 33, going on 34, I am so disappointed in myself for allowing my parents to influence such a major decision in my life. I can now only have a baby through in vitro fertilization.

Today my mom is different. As she's gotten older, her personality has softened and having distance between us been healthy. I think seeing me as a mom has also given her more respect for me in a way she seemed to struggle with prior to those life changes. Through therapy I've learned to radically accept her for who she is today and not who she used to be.

RANDOM RANT: Show of hands—who else's parents made them eat cereal with warmed milk because they believed if children drink cold things in the morning right after waking up it would make them sick. I know—whaaaat? My thoughts exactly. They would also only buy corn flakes and would allow us a pinch of sugar in your bowl so our teeth didn't rot—which I'm starting to think they genuinely believed that just one green apple Jolly Rancher and we'd be getting fitted for dentures!

Speaking of corn flakes—did you know that Kellogg's corn flake cereal was created to help people control their sexual urges?! Of course, the man who is the mastermind behind the bland breakfast choice, Dr. John Harvey Kellogg also believed in sterilizing people who he deemed as undesirable and may have dabbled a bit in eugenics. So definitely the kind of man you'd want to be getting sexual advice from or any advice for that matter.

Forever Golden

Like the comfort of an old blanket or the smell of your favorite book, my source of comfort ever since I was seven years old has been the famously hilarious classic sitcom The Golden Girls. I was first introduced to the show by my grandmother, whom I was visiting and meeting in Haiti for the first time. Having been raised in the states, I was nervous about how I was going to communicate with my grandmother, who only spoke Creole. I was raised speaking both English and Haitian Creole but living in America made English my strongest language.

We arrived in Mare Rouge, Haiti—the village where my mother was born and raised. My grandmother's house sat at the top of a hill surrounded by mountains covered in breathtakingly beautiful wild red flowers. Behind the house were palm trees and acres of wide-open greenery with chickens running around the yard. Just beyond that was a shallow waterfall that emptied into the crystal-clear ocean below.

When I saw my grandma, she greeted me with arms wide open, hugging and kissing me. She sat me on a big comfy royal blue loveseat facing the back window. Before I knew it, my grandma was clumsily lugging in an old-school tube TV. I smiled because I was under the impression there was no electricity in the village—let alone a TV that was only given power in the late afternoons for a few hours a day.

Grandma set it all up and sat down next to me. She explained we were going to watch "American TV" in her language. She winked and said in Creole, "I bet you've never seen that before! This is the TV your parents should be showing you to improve your Creole." As the grainy TV came to life and connected to the VCR—the theme song came on and I began giggling as Grandma sang along.

"Thank you for being a friend! Travel down the road and back again…" Her Haitian accent was strong, and I was in awe of her vivacity and laughter. She grabbed my hand and together we jumped around and danced to the rest of the theme song. We laughed uncontrollably, falling back into the couch and grabbing our bellies.

I'd never seen any other Haitian adult in my life be so silly and cavalier. I snuggled up to her as she explained this was her favorite episode and I watched in amazement as the voices of the Golden Girls: Dorothy, Blanche, Rose, and Sophia were replaced with Haitian women's voices, dubbed in Creole. I was hooked! After the episode was over, my grandma brought out a basket full of VHS tapes that were all dubbed into Creole episodes of The Golden Girls.

That week of my visit we watched hours of the funny TV series. Every now and then she'd interrupt our viewing with a snarky remark about the characters. She loved and connected with me in a way no one in my family ever has. We saw each other at least once every year when we'd go visit her in Haiti or vice versa. With every visit we'd engage in our tradition of watching The Golden Girls accompanied by a side of belly aching laughter and long conversations about life. She loved to tell me stories of my mother and her 11 siblings and always parted ways with me saying, "Keep smiling. Your gift is the happiness and comfort you bring to everyone you meet."

It was 2009 on September 3rd—my birthday—when I heard her say those words…for she knew it'd be the last time. I was honored to be her final call and, most importantly, had one last banter with her about our favorite television girls.

Though my nana is no longer here, I still watch at least one episode of The Golden Girls every night before I go to bed recalling her laughter and quirky ways. She gave me the confidence to be my unique self and reminded me of the power of laughter. I would not be the person I am today had she not been in my life. Gran, thank you for being a friend and the center of my heart.

Youth is fleeting. We often only truly begin to understand its purpose when we begin to lose our grip on it. The memories that make up the cells of your humanity and evolution slowly move from individual pockets of time to large chunks and moments. The lines blur and sway as we get older. What once used to be warm and familiar soon become distant memories that only show themselves in the moments that we think are just mundane.

By fifth grade, in our house, it was an unwritten but well understood rule that my siblings and I were never going to be part of the slumber party crew at school. However, though they were selective about who or when they'd allow us to have friends over, I did get to have sleepovers at my house with American kids. This only happened a handful of times so when I did get a "yes" I would waste no time in getting it all set up.

I made a new friend named Jessica who lived in my neighborhood. She was in my class and took the same walking-home route I did. Through many afternoons we'd walk the mile or so it took us to get home, gabbing and giggling about the school day, friends, and common enemies on the playground.

One weekend after going through all the typical parental hurdles set up by my parents, Jessica spent the night, and she partook in the usual events that filled my weekend like going to church with us on Sunday morning. We were fifth graders now so we were no longer infatuated with all things princess and frilly.

Clothes for me now were a statement and an expression of self. I was concerned about what I looked like and how others perceived me after years of being bullied for being Haitian, being short, being dark, or even having a high-pitched voice. Most importantly, I was no longer confined to my mother's homemade fashions, and it was freedom to be able to assemble my own looks. Whatever it was that would radiate the weird off me, I thought if only I looked, dressed and acted cool enough I could distract from all the things that made kids not like me or befriend me.

After church, Jessica and I walked to the mall while my parents were out still visiting with church friends. Though it wasn't the quickest walk, I genuinely figured at the time my parents would have no problem with us being out since we were using our own money and just wanted to browse and hang out.

Clearly Jo forgot for a minute who her parents were and was completely blind-sided when I arrived home and was met with an immediate backhanded slap from my dad as I walked through our front door. I was shocked and immediately turned to Jessica to see what she was feeling. Her mouth wide open, she watched with confusion and horror as my father irately screamed at me for walking to the mall about five minutes away from our house without his permission. Before I could say anything, he was threatening me with a whooping and shoving me into his bedroom. As the belt lashes fell harder and faster, the stinging burn of my skin made my screams excruciating and loud.

All I could think about was Jessica, standing outside the door and hearing the secrets I worked so hard to keep away from my peers. The beating grew more intense with screams so I willed myself to stop so my father's temper could let up and the whole thing could be over. He told me I deserved it for being out on my own with a white girl they didn't know that well yet.

My mom's voice cut through the commotion as she egged him on, ranting about how disrespectful I was being and how dare I make decisions as if I were grown. They double-teamed me with rhetorical questions like "What if you were kidnapped?" Or "What if you had been hit by a car?"

I begged for them to stop the humiliation and by the time it was over Jessica was sitting on the front stoop outside our house anxiously waiting for her mom to come pick her up. I apologized to her profusely and begged her not to mention this to anyone in school. Bewildered she searched for understanding by asking how often this happened and why was it happening at all. I had no answers for her and could only repeat weakly "please don't say anything."

She kept her promise and she never again spoke to me after what she witnessed. That was the last time I'd have any American friend spend the night in our home or over at all for that matter—and I was okay with it. A few years ago, Jessica popped up on a "possible people you may know" on my Facebook page. A little nervous, I requested her as a friend and to my surprise she quickly accepted and we began exchanging pleasantries via instant messaging and caught up on life after the fifth grade.

Jessica remembered me well and was still friendly. Still, I couldn't help but wonder if she remembered what happened. We kept it light and fluffy and I psyched myself out of asking her any further questions. Till this day, I am just too mortified that I even had to go through that, let alone in front of a stranger who was just getting to know me.

Because my childhood was filled with moments like this. I grew increasingly more controlling of my social life and even more quiet about what life was like for me at home. Having been through so much abuse I've normalized situations I assumed everyone experienced like I did.

That's the funny thing about trauma, the longer you live with it, the more likely you are to become desensitized to it. I was taught to keep my secrets buried and to hide my shame. Bottling up all that trauma is what led to more abusive situations and heightened my anxiety over the years.

Today it shows itself in how I love and who I love. My anger issues run so deep that most of my time is spent trying to manage it and my mental health. I have a lot to be angry about, but I don't wish to be angry forever. I only yearn to be heard and understood. I only wish to be free of my traumas and burdens.

Chapter 12 ~ Simply Complicated

"Feet, what do I have you for when I have wings to fly..."

~Frida Khalo

To own a home as a first-generation immigrant was the pinnacle of what it meant to Haitian people to achieve the "American dream"—at least in the 80s, 90s, and early 2000s. Today's Gen Z's population/community who are just tasting the flavors life has to offer have been privileged enough to have a couple of generations ahead of them to measure their life perspectives up against.

I am a proud millennial and am one through and through. I grew up in the dot com era and am very blessed to have been given such a leap in life than the generations before me who didn't have knowledge at the tip of their fingers. We're blessed to live in a modern world where we could simply type our random thoughts into the Google search bar and be immediately enlightened with a plethora of knowledge, facts, views, and opinions that are endless and can certainly drive you mad if you let them.

I was maybe ten or eleven when I was first given access to a computer at home that could connect to the internet. That's right! Dial-up! Unlike Lorelai Gilmore who had hollered through the phone at her endlessly aggravating, uppity mother in Season 1 of Gilmore Girls—I was not as allured by the slow, molasses feeling that seemed to go hand in hand with this sudden ability to have all your unanswered questions answered.

Starting with an AOL account that Lanau introduced me to when we first started dating—I quickly learned how much freedom and access the internet gives you. I was taken by the origins of instant messaging through chat rooms and being able to purchase something within minutes of finally getting that website's page to load up—giving you the ability to read and research to your heart's content.

Call me a nerd or whatever, but I absolutely LOVE research and learning new things! I couldn't see myself right now happily going back to the scrutiny and alien-like takeover of my academic years—especially the college years that had on my life—in my heart I will forever be a seeker of knowledge. Up until I officially hung up my hat in the student world and picked up my new attire masqueraded as the "adult world"—I remained fascinated by the written word in all its forms and power to change our outlook on life within moments of consuming it.

Before Google, I had encyclopedias—which I'll admit had a certain level of comfort and credibility. Fact-checking was a new concept, and it was very difficult for my young and impressionable mind to understand that as grand, official, or scholarly as the internet may seem—there are still pockets of unknown truths that are just pining to lead you astray.

As a kid, I often hid or masked my love for random facts and research, fearing to be called what it is that other people around my age summed up to be weird and unseemly. I loved books, magazines, and just about any medium in those days that gave way to an escape from my everyday life. I remember feeling this immense pressure to always be the best and that, in my head, required being as smart as possible and absorbing as much knowledge as possible.

I enjoy watching. documentaries on things as random as the history of toilets and human hygiene, to the way crayons are made to the compelling history of the Vikings. I love reading about the Victorian Era and people who once were. From the captivating details of the murders committed by Lizzie Borden to dissecting the scattered and tortured mind of Edgar Allan Poe. I've researched the Black Panthers, Fred Hampton, Malcolm X, and the civil rights movement. I regularly find myself immersed in the fascination of figures like Billie Holiday, Marilyn Monroe, and Judy Garland. I liked to think of how these figures contributed to our history. I loved to understand their minds and absorb their wisdom like a sponge.

Knowing others' stories and collecting random knowledge is a high like no other for me. It makes me feel good and keeps me in an ever-learning cycle. You never know when it'll be essential to whip out your knowledge of Van Gogh's afflicted psyche in comparison to Sylvia Plath's psychosis. Or debate the scattered mind of Queen Elizabeth I as she unknowingly poisoned herself to death over her notorious and incessant need to cake lead-based makeup on her face that gradually ate away at her flesh and killed her.

My dad, though limited in his access to education throughout his life, always made certain we knew that intelligence was a skill—a muscle that must be regularly challenged and reevaluated through fresh lenses and education. As we get older our memories begin to shrink in their clarity. Years rather swiftly turn into blurry chunks of decades once lived. We no sooner forget the smell of our first resting place as we pick up new nuggets of knowledge and information—almost like you must trade clear and vibrant memories to make room for the essential and most meaningful.

Today, I continue to keep an always-growing list of things I want to research and know more about. Each piece of knowledge lets me in on a little sneak peek of what it's like to thoroughly know who you are as a person and what you stand for. It took me a while to realize that much like my writings in this book, at the root of any formidable concept stands a flawed human being who just got lucky with an epiphany.

We're never more than a few pensive and analytical thoughts away from the next big thing. It's an art that continues to be underrated. Tell your children to dream and imagine because those small ideas lead to big ones that will ultimately make up who they become.

Words have the power to break, cut, heal, influence, and even kill the core of our humanity. Our language houses our innermost thoughts and beliefs. Near my mid-thirties and I still find joy in the small epiphanies. For no one will ever truly know you, as you know yourself. Knowledge IS a superpower. Indulge in it as much as you can, while you can.

> *White Christianity suffers from a bad case of Disney princess theology. As each individual reads scripture, they see themselves as the process in every story. They are Esther, never Xerxes or Haman. They are Peter, but never Judas. They are the woman anointing Jesus, never the*

Pharisees. They are the Jews escaping slavery, never Egypt. For citizens of the most powerful country in the world, who enslaved both Native and Black people, to see itself as Israel and Egypt when studying scripture is a perfect example of Disney princess theology. It means that as people in power, they have no lens for locating themselves rightly in scripture or society—and it has made them blind and utterly ill-equipped to engage in issues of power and injustice. It is some very weak bible work.

~Erna Kim Hackett

Christianity and Me

I've avoided talking about this one because Lord knows I am ACUTELY aware of where I currently live, the army of white saviors surrounding me and the people I grew up with. But at the risk of pissing many off—here we go! #unapologeticliving

See, what most people don't know about me (at least those who didn't grow up with me and who are well aware of what I'm referring to) is that I accepted Jesus Christ as my personal savior when I was 15. It's a moment I'll never forget. It was the day I decided to separate myself from religion and commit to my spiritual relationship with God.

I realized the performative nature of those who claimed to be Christians. I even recognized it in myself. Truthfully, as a child, Christianity was just my ticket to gaining the ultimate approval and love I yearned for from my parents.

As they grew stronger in their faith, so did our activities and presence as a family at church. I wanted to impress them and make them proud SO BAD—and they knew it.

A good two years later after being saved, that perfect image of "the church" that I'd grown so attached to was demolished. We'd been part of the same church most of my life and many of the members became extended family. Being the daughter of a deacon turned pastor, the church was as natural to me as breathing.

Again—"Lekol, leglize, lakay!" Meaning this WAS your life until that fateful day you got to strike out on your own and just LIVE according to you. When it was all taken away, so was the veil that somehow covered up the humans I had put up on this pedestal and proclaimed Godly to the point of perfection.

The imperfection I now saw clear as day, made me question everything. I questioned the idea of "the church." I questioned my parents who of course could never be wrong, and I questioned myself. When life began to happen to me in my late teens, I felt lost. I felt like my identity had been stolen and I couldn't imagine a world without my "routine."

Life flowed into my early twenties and so much had happened to me, I shut out the world and retreated inward. I had been sick, suffered multiple miscarriages and just felt broken.

One evening I locked myself in my bedroom and I had it out with God. LITERALLY. I was angry. I felt damaged and I didn't understand why. For hours I wrote furiously in my journal and cried uncontrollably. Tired and through sore eyes, I stared outside the window into the darkness when the words of Cece Winan's "For Love Alone" started playing in my head. It was a gospel song that had really resonated with me when I was 15 and was just beginning to really understand the difference between being religious and spiritual.

Grabbing my laptop, I quickly got onto YouTube and typed in the song title. Listening to the lyrics I smiled, sang, danced, and worshipped right there in the safety of my first apartment's bedroom. I had never experienced this wholeness before.

> *"For love alone, I live my life.*
> *And from this moment on I vow to never lose sight.*
> *If I ever doubt the reasons why I'm here,*
> *I'll start questioning my fears and know it's for love alone."*

I must have listened to it fifty times that evening and a million times since. It's become my life's anthem and the anchor to my true self. What I gained that evening was my spirituality and my unwavering connection to God. In my darkest moments, he preserved my life and reminded me what it's all about and what it's always been about for me— LOVE.

I no longer refer to myself as anything but a woman who knows love because of the love God has shown me and it had nothing to do with the labels, or that building, or competing to see who could "appear more Godly." I'm a flawed human being and because I removed myself from those expectations, I've come to know the real me and that needed no validation.

I've been to different churches since but it's no longer something I feel obligated to be a part of. Much like living at home with my parents, moving to Alexandria was the same in the way people shoved church and religion down your throat. If you're not part of the church crowd here, you're immediately alienated and made to feel like a terrible person for not being part of the Christian faith.

It never gets old watching the look of utter confusion spread across someone's face when you meet them for the first time in town and reply with "I don't go to church" to their presumptive questioning of what church you belong to.

I despise the pressure of being picked apart and feeling like you must uphold a certain way of life to fit in with "these people." I hate when my real-life problems and experiences are dismissed into this whirlwind of toxic positivity and blind faith that allows people to sit in their disillusion and complacency.

It stops being about my soul but rather just living up to others' standards, in fear of being seen as "Un-Christian" or worse, being shunned from people you've allowed into your heart. So understand, it's nothing personal when I turn down your billionth invitation to your church. Dude, it's honestly just not for me.

I've had my fair share of awful experiences to know that that world isn't good for my mental health or my spirit— which I will protect at all cost. I'm so grateful for the unique Haitian church experience I had growing up because it was and IS incomparable to any other! Church in the Haitian world is a WHOLE party y'all! Full band and everything! We don't sit still and hum.

Growing up in the church has shaped so much of who I am and has kept me connected to my Haitian family and roots. It brought me some of my best friendships that still exist today because of the life we all shared as being the weird

Haitian church kids growing up in a tiny, NOSEY Haitian community—smack dab in the middle of an American world.

It's funny because people here in Alexandria think that I'm just another lost soul who needs saving—not knowing that after an entire childhood of memorizing and reciting scripture competitively for sport, I could probably run circles around you in that biblical trivia—like down to a science.

To those of you who are still clutching your pearls, CHILL boo. I swear I'm not dancing naked under a full moon or whipping up potions in my kitchen! My spiritual life is just none of your damn bid-ness.

When you're the weird Haitian kid around, friendships just didn't come easily. I always had "friends" but I've only had a few genuine friendships over my life span so far. Looking different and sounding different always made me stand out, and not in the best way. Kids weren't clamoring at the chance to speak to me, so much as they were ready to make me the butt of their jokes and meanness.

Mynoucka, Faye, and Gertrude were the only true friends I had as a child and well into my late teen years we remained extremely close. After years of being picked on, I didn't feel the need to go searching for more friends and thus, never really learned how to make friends beyond our little clique of Haitian church kids.

With the girls, however, I needed no excuses or explanation. We just got each other and it didn't work. On weekends when my mother wouldn't allow me to go to their houses until I did chores, the girls would sometimes come over and help me get my chores done in hopes of having a little bit of time to hang out with me.

We all met at different times around the ages of 6 and 8. Mynoucka, Gertrude and I were all the same ages, though Mynoucka was a year ahead of us both in school. Faye was two years older than all of us and naturally became the big sister of the group. My relationship with all of them was different and evolved drastically throughout our childhood and teen years.

Mynoucka was my closest friend and I considered her my best friend for quite some time. She was the first one of the girls I met when my family first started attending services at First Haitian Baptist Church in Fort Myers. She was the popular girl in church and by the way adults spoke of her you would've thought she was the second coming of Christ! The big story was that she had survived a really bad accident. When she was a toddler, she was hit by a car. Being so small doctors believed she was lucky to have survived the accident.

The story made her the 'it' girl that all the adults doted on and all the kids, including myself, were envious of. She seemed to have it all, know it all and do it all. She wore the best clothes and had the best hairstyles. She spoke, read, and wrote creole fluently and performed by singing and dancing at church all the time. She was well-known to be a super smart student in school and during Bible competitions at the church, she was always the first to memorize her scriptures and win first place—which were typically cash prizes.

My parents quickly became friends with her mother and the occasional visits to Mynoucka's house made me want nothing more than to be her friend. She was the first friend

I ever knew who didn't have a dad and was raised solely by her mother who remained single most of her life. As I got to know her and we became friends, I learned she was so much more than we kids thought her to be. While she had nice things and she was also incredibly humble and was just a super sweet girl. She made me feel important and I never thought she'd befriend me of all people.

Mynoucka and I went through middle school and high school together, always remaining thick as thieves. We maintained our little girl group at church, and it was always something that bonded us. We later brought in Faye and Gertrude to be part of our little gospel group and it kept us tethered together for years.

Not too long after I met Mynoucka, I met Gertrude and we became fast friends. Gertrude and Mynoucka are actually cousins through marriage. Gertrude was and still is one of the most profound souls I've ever met in my life. She was not only beautiful but she was always wise beyond her years. As we grew into our teen years, Gertrude became the friend I often leaned on for comfort. Quick to forgive and not at all judgmental, she always affirmed me as being better than I thought of myself.

Faye and I met through our parents who were so close. My mother and father were the best man and matron of honor at her mother's wedding to her stepdad. Our families being so close made us practically family ourselves. We went to the same schools along with her little brother Rony who was about two years younger than me. For a while we believed we were cousins until our parents had sudden falling out. Something that often happened when my parents were friends or got close to anyone.

During those years that they weren't speaking, our parents

kept us from hanging out together and it wouldn't be until Faye was a teenager and I was a preteen would we reunite despite our parents' issues with one another.

As the girls and I grew into young women, we began developing our independence and growing in our vastly different personalities. I started becoming more comfortable with who I was and was not afraid to be the different one. At one point this made me feel insecure. I imagined they'd grow up and all remain friends without me.

While I wasn't entirely incorrect in that fear, I've come to realize that we would've grown apart for the most part. They were all looking to become nurses and part of the medical field and I remained the dreamer who simply wanted to write and create. Even as a teen who barely knew herself, I always knew writing would forever be part of my life.

By the time we were all dating boys who all happen to be friends, we learned very quickly that our innocent days of singing, dancing, and vegging out on Papa John's pizza were long behind us. Though most of the relationships didn't survive, Lanau and I did. Once BabyGate was upon us, they had a difficult time watching me make choices they felt were hurting me.

By this time, I was completely and madly in love with Lanau and trusted our relationship over everything else that was in my life. I showed him sides and parts of me I'd never had the balls to show or be open about with the girls. As the cheating years went down, the distance grew further in our friendships, and we soon began to look beyond the four of us as friends.

After all those years of ups and downs with Lanau in Fort

Myers, I couldn't wait to leave. I shut everyone out of our relationship and began keeping the details of our relationship to myself and from the girls. By the time Lanau and I were in a healthy and stable place, the girls didn't know our story and didn't really support the fact that we were still together, even after having taken a break from one another in the Fall of 2007.

Still, even throughout our 20s, Mynoucka, Gertrude, Faye and I remained staples in one another's lives. We showed up for the big moments and tried to be there for one another as best we can. Mynoucka and Gertrude went on to be nurses, though Gertrude has switched her focus to being a mom after having her son a couple years ago with another on the way!

Faye followed her heart and is making her way in the fashion world as a stylist—something I knew she was always meant to do. As a girl group she would style us for performances and would put all our outfits together. She too is now a mommy and wife.

They're all still women of faith and if anything, have only gone deeper and deeper into their faith. As expected, I've remained the wild child, free spirit I've always been. I don't live a conventional life and I am a walking mound of contradictions—and I wouldn't have it any other way.

Friends Like These

As the girls and I began drifting apart because we were all on different educational paths, I became very close with a fellow Haitian queen, Katie. We were both about 19 when Katie and I began getting close. I'd only recently begun hearing about her through whispers and rumors from other Haitian kids in town. Based on the rumors about her you would've thought she must eat babies for breakfast.

Katie wasn't at all like the other Haitian teens our age. She was completely independent and was an emancipated, former foster kid. Katie didn't play the same rules in life as so many of us Haitian church kids and most of the hate she got was from the fact that most people were just jealous of her lifestyle and seemingly grown and free lifestyle.

Katie worked a full-time job, lived on her own, and seemed to be her own person—free of the grips of domineering Haitian parents. Hell, I envied her life and couldn't wait to just sample a taste of that level of freedom and independence. All the girls wanted to be her and all the boys wanted to date her.

I first heard of Katie from Mynoucka who had a complicated relationship with her throughout the years. Our boyfriends were all in awe of Katie and some people even made comparisons between Mynoucka and Katie's looks. They were both beautiful and for the most part had their pick of boys both Haitian and American who would gladly drop everything to date them.

Being who I was, having the goody-two-shoes reputation I had and coming from the family I did, I assumed a girl like Katie would never want or care to be friends with me. As she got closer to Mynoucka, Faye and Gertrude—we continually found ourselves in each other's presence.

From what I could tell, Katie was a complete sweetheart and not at all conniving as so many of our peers made her out to be. I admired her because I was given the opportunity to see a side of Katie very few ever had the honor of seeing. She was driven, ambitious, super smart, and seemed to just always have it all figured out. While most of us as teens barely had access to money due to menial part-time work or not having any money at all. Most of us were still dependent on our parents so to us, Katie was living that grown and sexy life we all were dying to attain for ourselves.

As we grew in our friendship, we began spending real time together and I was fascinated by the life she'd led up until that point. While others seen her as this lucky chick who had it made, I learned she was an abandoned and neglected child who very quickly became a product of the system within just a couple of years from the time she immigrated to the states to live with her mother's family.

Not having a mother or a father there to look out for her and advocate for her well-being, Katie had to grow up fast and quickly learned to be her own parent. Bouncing from one foster home to the next between the ages of 9 and 17 when she was officially granted emancipation—Katie endured many traumas at the hand of adults who were supposed to be looking out for her. It all began to make sense as to why she put up such a tough girl exterior and was very reluctant to allow others into her heart.

Shortly after becoming friends, Katie unexpectedly found

herself pregnant. Even though I knew she was scared and alone with a baby on the way, she handled the whole situation gracefully—even when her pregnancy turned out to be a high-risk one due to some complications the baby was having in utero. I wanted to be there for her in any way that I could and we spent most of her pregnancy hanging out together. We ate together. We laughed together. We even cried together. The idea of being a single mother weighed heavy on her conscience the entire pregnancy and she often felt guilty bringing a child into a two-parent home.

But I kept reminding her how strong she was and that I knew she had the ability to do this on her own and still follow her dreams—which—spoiler alert! That's exactly what she did and then some! Katie delivered a beautiful baby boy in February of 2008. I had just moved to Tampa for college and due to the baby's special medical needs, she was set to deliver him at the children's hospital in St. Petersburg, Florida, which was only a 45-minute drive from my new college apartment.

Though I wasn't able to be there because I had to be in classes, Faye was there for Katie during the delivery and made sure she was not alone the entire day. Because the baby had open heart surgery right after he was born, he was in the hospital for the first four to five months of his life in the ICU.

Katie didn't need anyone though and her son had everything he needed within his very determined, no-bullshit mother. Being a single mother didn't deter or hinder Katie's educational and career plans at all. Though she struggled at times, she put herself through college and earned a BA in social work, and a master's in criminology. Steadily building her career, Katie started out as a social worker, then became a case manager and eventually, made the even more courageous decision to become a police officer and join the police academy.

I watched Katie go through hell and back over the years and though we never did end up living in the same city again, we remained friends and only grew closer with the distance. At 33, Katie is the longest running, most consistent and solid friendship I've had in my whole life. We could go months on end and never hear from one another and within a single phone call, we can catch up and feel like we were never apart.

She's the friend who has been there no matter what, and even when we had clashes in our past, we never allowed our friendship to fall apart. Katie understands me on a level no one outside of my husband and therapist knows me. Her son is my Godson and I am never not grateful that we've had each other to lean on all these years.

Knowing my obsession with *Golden Girls*, she recently joked about how we just may end up living together in our golden years, still—in the famous words of daytime celebrity news talk show host, Wendy Williams—"dippin' and doin' it" like we're still 19-years-old. Being in my 30s, I now know how rare friendships like ours are. I'm blessed to still have my Katie in my life.

I've been blessed to have friends who love me as I am. After I moved to Tampa for college, it took me a while to accept the fact that I had to actually make an effort to make friends if I wanted any semblance of a good college experience.

Merida was the first friend I made in Tampa. We both worked as customer service associates at Bed, Bath &

Beyond and when we met, we clicked instantly. Merida is Dominican and our liking to each other started over the appreciation and understanding we had of each other's cultures. We were both the children of first-generation immigrants and no one understood being a disappointment to our parents like we did.

Merida was chill and just an absolute comfort to be with. I think she is easily one of the most beautiful women I've ever seen in my life. She even has a heart of gold to match. We could talk about anything from world issues and culture to love and a shared affinity for trap music we could shake our ass and whine our hips to.

As I moved into different parts of my career, I took Merida with me and soon we were spending everyday together, carpooling to work together, having lunch together—we even reserved our weekends to party together along with our boyfriends, now husbands. Merida is the kind of friend that even if it's two o'clock in the morning, if you need her, she's there—no questions asked.

My favorite and best memories in Tampa include Merida and I miss her energy being around me all the time. She taught me to be daring, confident and not to give zero fucks. She's always a party and I can't think of a bored moment we've ever shared outside of endless workdays. Like Katie and the girls, Merida will always be a permanent friend in my life.

In college, I made friends with lots of different people because I lived in college housing where my roommates were matched with me based on personality forms that we all completed when we signed the lease to live there. For the most part, my roommates were fine but every now and again, I ran into that one weird or crazy roommate that made me wonder why I chose to live in a place where my roommates were liable to change every few months!

I had a roommate whose boyfriend used to steal and eat my food—even the meals I cooked and left on the stove! I had another roommate whose personality and style changed with every new guy she introduced us to. I still can't definitively remember who she was for real because she was that whatever-you-need-me-to-be girl. I had another roommate who lived with her boyfriend for a short period of time for one summer. Every Tuesday night, the two would get all dressed up in the exact same rat-pack/pinup girl themed outfits, left the apartment at two in the morning exactly and would return together just before seven that morning. Their outfits never changed, and they never deviated from that two to seven a.m. block.

One of my very first roommates Erin was in the navy and graduated as a nuclear captain. We loved staying up at night and talking about our lives. She was such a genuine person and had the sweetest soul. We remained friends long after we stopped living together.

In fact, Lanau and I's very first vacation together as a couple was to Waikiki, Hawaii where Erin was stationed at Pearl Harbor. She invited us to stay in her condo that overlooked the mountains and the breathtakingly beautiful Waikiki Beach. It was the most remarkable trip we'd both ever been on and Erin was a major reason why we were able to afford to go on it in our early 20s.

Leneah was the roommate that I became the closest to in all my years of college housing. After we lived together, we maintained our friendship and she was my maid of honor when Lanau and I got married. Today she is a successful accountant who lives in Panama with her handsome husband and adorable baby girl. Leneah taught me what it meant to live in the moment and how to accept nothing less than ultimate happiness.

Faye, Gertrude, Mynoucka & Me

Katie & Me

Merida & Me

Leneah & Me

Chapter 13 ~ Just Call Me Boo Radley

"I would build my world which while I lived, would be in agreement with all the worlds. The day, or the hour, or the minute that I lived would be mine and everyone else's—my madness would not be an escape from 'reality.'"

~Frida Khalo

The decision to move to Minnesota was really made out of desperation. Our little family was under complete financial distress in Florida, and we knew our next step would be crucial and take every ounce of faith I had to do what was best for our son, who was a year old at the time. By the end of the summer of 2015, we'd lost our jobs and our home, so we needed to make a jump.

For years my husband's brother had been urging us to come to Minnesota and give it a chance. Being from Florida himself, he was well aware of the depleting job market and the growing cost of living there. He had been a resident of Alexandria for about a decade at the time, so we felt fairly confident in our ability to make it work here from a financial standpoint. His wife at the time, Michelle, agreed with John and knew we'd have a better chance of stabilizing our lives there rather than in Florida. Before we knew it, she was sending us airline tickets and just like that, our lives were shifting in ways we did not anticipate, nor were we ready for.

The plan was to come north for about six months, build up some money, and go back to the lives we'd left behind. We arrived in Alexandria in August 2015, and I was overwhelmed with how different Alexandria was in comparison to what we were used to in Florida.

Yes, it was a total culture shock. Tampa is incredibly diverse, and my being a dark-skinned Haitian American woman there was not out of the ordinary. My looks, including my skin tone, plus the way I speak and my worldview aligned with my peers back home. But Alexandria was like walking into a time-warp. In the early years my husband and I would laugh over our misery in feeling like we lived on the set of To Kill a Mockingbird and we were Boo Radley.

Sure, the town was beautiful as I'd imagined it would be but the energy of indifference and disdain that radiated off the town's people was palpable. I had never in my life been so acutely aware of my skin color until I moved to Alexandria. In a way, it created an insecurity I never knew I had or could have. Suddenly, my family and I stood out uncomfortably and my husband was viewed as threatening.

Consciously, and/or perhaps subconsciously at times, many residents of Alexandria let me know how different I am to them. From the long stares to the blunt open questions including, "Where are you from?" and "Why are you here?" and even, "When are you planning to leave?"

Nearly six years later, I still feel pressured to answer these questions. Being an introvert, this is a completely unnerving experience for me. However, living here in Alexandria has forced me to come to terms with my fears and insecurities. I am proud to be a Black woman and even prouder to be a Haitian American Black woman. If anything, it's taught me to appreciate the very things that make me stand out. Since moving to Minnesota, I have learned a great deal about basic human kindness and the reach it has.

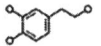

Before moving to Alexandria, I was fairly naïve to blatant discrimination on a personal level. It lingered in the shadows of my upbringing and early adult years. It had just never landed squarely on my doorstep. I had become numb to the occasional rude comments made by store clerks, or to an overly eager salesperson who seemed all-too-anxious to become my shopping shadow. While I had been schooled in the concepts of racial discrimination, most of it was politically correct, watered-down African American history. It was difficult to personalize it as a Haitian American.

Difficulty quickly turned to shock when I moved to Alexandria. I was taken aback by hurtful instances showing a complete lack of basic human respect and kindness. I wasn't expecting this from the land of "Minnesota Nice."

On one occasion, I was taking my daughter to Alexandria Clinic for a checkup. I was on the main lobby floor, loading my baby into the elevator. An elderly couple stood outside the door, and as I held it open with my feet, I leaned over to ask them if I should hold it open. They ignored me. I asked again, in case they had not heard me the first time. The woman glanced over at me with a look of disgust, then quickly turned her stare back to the wall ignoring me. Just then, I realized what the issue was and stepped back, waiting for the elevator doors to close.

As the awkward silence washed over us, a man who was nearby must have witnessed the exchange and came running in. He quickly jammed the button to close the doors. Panting hard from the dash, he looked over at me and said, "I'm so sorry, ma'am." Still catching his breath, he continued, "That was just so uncalled for."

"It's okay," I said, chuckling a bit to make light of the situation. "I'm getting used to it."

He sighed deeply, "That's the problem. You shouldn't have to get used to it." At that moment, I thought about what had just happened and I was sad and a bit ashamed for feeling I had to accommodate others for their ignorance. This was certainly not the first, second, or even third time this had happened, nor would it be the last. The intensity deepened.

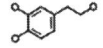

#WalkingWhileBlack

The exhaustion that's felt by my family within a racist community isn't just exhausting. It's a daily mental battle to constantly be made aware of your skin and the boundaries it creates. Where Lanau and I once used to enjoy long walks on the beach back home in Florida or just being poolside with our sun—these activities have now become almost nonexistent in my life.

Taking walks for my family and I is now a privilege. When we go out as a family now, we have to be conscious of what we look like or what we are wearing. Even with our little boy and girl in tow—we're careful not to look lingering at any homes as we pass by. We even go as far as making sure we're all wearing bright colors—anything to distract from the blackness of our skin that can lead to possible conflict.

And yet, even after taking all these precautions, we still get stared at or have people coming out of their homes as if to warn us "I see you." Isn't that wild?! That a simple stroll around the neighborhood would require so much thought? But that's our reality.

It doesn't matter that we're upstanding citizens who are actively involved in the community. It doesn't matter what organization's board we sit on, or what careers we have. I can't take away what they perceive as a "threat," any more than we can change this skin we live in that compels them into such fear. I just look forward to the day when I can reply to "Do you want to go for a walk?" with a simple "Yeah. Let's go!"

This piece was the first speech I ever gave as an adult. It was to a large group of Alexandrians only weeks after

George Floyd was murdered in the Twin Cities (Minneapolis)—truly changing the world and our level of self-awareness. The spring and summer of 2020 permanently changed the way people perceive one another. It tore into our most vulnerable spaces and made us feel weak and broken.

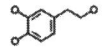

No, THIS Is America

A few nights ago, my husband and I were putting our two kids down for bed. As I reached over my six-year-old son with the blanket to tuck him in, he asked me quietly, "Mommy, is the police going to come to kill me and my daddy?" Falling to my knees beside his bed, my eyes welled with tears and overflowed as my heart sank into the pit of my stomach. I stared into his little eyes, desperately searching my mind for the right words to say when his dad came over, sat on the side of his bed, and said, "Hey Buddy, as long as you're here with us, you're always safe. Go to sleep. No worries. You're home with your family."

This moment with our son was one we knew many little black boys and girls all over our country tonight were experiencing, going to bed with the same inquiries racing through their minds. About two days before this exchange, news broke of an unarmed black man in Minneapolis who was brutally murdered by police officers. In a video taken by a witness, we saw three of them kneeling on the man's body while one of them pressed his knee firmly into the back of the man's neck for nearly nine minutes, capturing the horrific scene as the world watched him take his final breaths.

This past February a black man in Georgia, while jogging in broad daylight, was killed by two white men who claimed to be carrying out a "citizen's arrest" #AhmaudArbery. Within two days of that breaking news, we lost yet another black soul in Texas, this time a woman, #BreonnaTaylor, who was shot dead in her sleep when three officers, dressed in civilian clothing, kicked in the door of her home while executing a "no-knock warrant." They realized later it was one giant mistake, as the person the officers were looking for had already been detained elsewhere. Less than a week later #GeorgeFloyd is killed—all this whilst the black community is being disproportionately affected by COVID-19 and dying by the thousands due to our community's lack of access to proper healthcare. George Floyd's murder, for the black community, was the straw that broke the camel's back.

Being a black woman in a white homogenous community means I am never not aware of my blackness and what it portrays to those around me. I spend a great deal of time and energy being conscious of what I look like, how I sound, what I wear, what's in my hands or even how I'm being perceived when I'm around white people. In the black community we refer to this as "code-switching." It's essentially our daily checklist of overcoming black stereotypes that have been assigned to people of color in our society. I even go so far as to monitor my reactions and emotions, always making sure I am never labeled as "threatening" or "angry." What's sad is that I know I have an advantage as a woman because I have seen the even greater lengths my husband, a black man, has taken to ensure he's never deemed as threatening by his mere presence.

Frankly, to be black in America is exhausting. We don't have the privilege of "not seeing color" because the world rarely misses an opportunity to remind us that our white counterparts certainly do—even those who seem completely unaware of their own implicit biases and privilege. To "not see color" is to dismiss the existence of an entire race along with their centuries of pain, oppression, and generational trauma. The fact that my six-year-old son is already aware of his own blackness is validation that the cycle continues and now, more than ever, it's imperative that we break it.

I can't change the nature of the world around him any more than he can change his beautiful melanin skin. It's a reality I'm forced to radically accept. Regardless of your politics or world views, what we can all agree on is that no child should ever feel fearful that they're going to one day be killed simply for existing. The whole concept makes my heart ache and I'm consistently flip-flopping from outraged to deeply hurt to wishing people could just try to understand.

As Americans it is no longer enough to just stand by and hope things will get better. As a wife and mother of black men, I urge you to challenge yourself to imagine what it must be like to be black in a world that will feverishly look for any excuse to justify why a black man, and sometimes a woman or children, had to die. Time and time again as people go unpunished for these evil and savage acts, we're reminded that we live in a nation that sees us as disposable. Whether you're inclined to believe it or not, the black community is under attack. We're fighting a war that was waged four hundred years ago when our ancestors were kidnapped from their lands, stripped, shaved, and shackled like animals onto a ship. Can you imagine?

Men, women and children alike were starved for weeks, barely surviving the dangerous voyage into a foreign world.

Can you imagine? Literally tagged and branded "niggers," a term that was meant to rid them of their identity, they were propped up on a podium—only to be sold to the highest bidder. Can you imagine? Their value wasn't based on their intelligence or what they'd accomplished. Like cattle, it was based on how strong they were physically, whether they were capable of producing children, or could handle hard labor. One day you're an individual and the next you're just part of the livestock. Slaves were forbidden to keep their own names, their own cultures, and their own languages—their humanity. Can you imagine?

Today with our modern comforts, freedom, and independence, it's easy to dismiss a world we feel long detached. We do ourselves a disservice in failing to see the various moving parts and complexities that have systematically upheld and redefined what human bondage looks like in our country. Like a virus, it continues to permeate and exist within every orifice of our society. It exists in our justice system, entertainment, politics, and even within our schools. As a collective, my community has had enough. We just cannot continue to deny what is right before us.

Allyship is our only way forward. All lives cannot matter if black lives don't matter. We as people have a fundamental right to moving the needle forward and ending the trauma of millions of people across the globe. This time—it's personal. This time you don't have to be of color to relate to the human suffering that is taking place all around us. We have to acknowledge the hate and violence that's been unleashed on the black race. We have to find a way to get there—not only for us, and not just for our children, but for the future of all mankind. **Say their names!**

Allyship is a lifelong process of building relationships based on trust, consistency, and accountability with marginalized individuals and/or groups of people. Not self-defined—work and efforts must be recognized by those you are seeking to ally with.

After George Floyd was murdered in late May of 2020, my husband and I suffered quietly amongst ourselves—knowing we were surrounded by a community of people who for the most part could not have cared less about the protests taking place in the Twin Cities, let alone the alarming number of Black and Brown people who were being killed by police. This is how I felt at the height of the protests and couldn't help but to post a cathartic Facebook rant, with a liberal use of exclamation marks and colorful language:

I'm sorry. I am through seeing the whining of White people about the riots! You really don't fucking get it do you?! We ARE LITERALLY BEING PUBLICLY EXECUTED by YOUR PEOPLE! The ones who are only there to "protect and serve" YOU...NOT US! Where were all the MLK peaceful bullshit two weeks ago when crowds of WHITE MEN were storming a fucking FEDERAL BUILDING WITH GUNS!!! Where was the fucking tear gas, huh?! Did you forget your vast knowledge of Dr. King's sayings then?! Or does it only apply to us?

There are good cops—no argument and duh! One of my best friends in Florida is a cop and a Black woman at that! But THIS right here is not about them. It's about the RACIST fucks who permeate the system, giving the good ones a bad name by pronouncing themselves judge, jury, and executioner. It's about the ones who walk around with hate in their hearts for Black and Brown people of ANY KIND and hiding in plain sight behind a badge!

If your WHITE BROTHERS, FATHERS, HUSBANDS, and SONS were being treated this way with no one being brought to justice over and over and over again, only to be told "well they should've done this" or "they shouldn't have done that"—any excuse to justify why yet another Black person had to die for simply fucking existing! I mean, are you stressing trying to find words to convince your six-year-old son that policemen aren't going to kill him or his dad, and that he shouldn't be fearful when you, yourself know there's SO MUCH to be fearful about?!

One day his cuteness will expire and he'll cross over to "threatening" with a target on his back. Is your version of the "birds and the bees" talk a sad sit-down? While we're teaching our kids how not to react, dress, look, talk, or even sound when dealing with police and authorities?! ALL THIS—in hopes that the advice will one day save their lives?!

NO. There's YOUR America and then there's OURS and it's a traumatic reality we have to wrestle with every single day just trying to survive in YOUR WHITE world. You know, the one that was only built with YOUR race in mind. Y'all can miss me with all that! This is 1000% a Black and White issue—pun intended! I welcome you to make liberal use of your "unfriend" button because I WILL NOT STOP POSTING, WRITING, or SPEAKING ABOUT IT UNTIL WE START TO SEE ACTUAL CHANGE! No one wants to be in this position but here we are! Deal! #BLACKLIVESMATTER #whitefragility I said, what I said! Periodt! Thank you for stopping by.

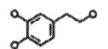

The spring of 2019 was a major shift in my life in

Alexandria. It was the end of April and in less than four months, my life took on a whole new identity. I decided to trust my heart and go with what I now know to have always been my purpose. After years of living like a virtual recluse, I found myself really wanting to step out of my comfort zone and reclaim my power of being in control of my own fate and life.

I hopped on Google and began researching 'Toastmasters," an organization that helps you practice public speaking, improve communication proficiency and build leadership skills. As I've shared before, I suffer from anxiety, so standing in front of a crowd and delivering speeches and speaking to a group of people was not exactly my forte.

Nevertheless, I hunted for a public speaking event, and ultimately, landed on a flier for a local speaking event happening at the local college. I'd recently reconnected with Deb LeDoux who was the chair of an organization called the Inclusion Network, we had met the summer before when I submitted my story of experiencing racism and discrimination in Alexandria since moving here only a couple years before.

After quite a few months of skillfully dodging her emails inviting me to various Inclusion Network meetings—I finally took Deb up on her offer to usher me into the event and introduce me to people she'd been telling me about for months and were great people to have in my corner.

The event was being sponsored by the Inclusion Network itself. Deb was never too pushy—always assuring me the Inclusion Network was a safe space. She was excited that I'd decided to attend the event and felt it was going to be a positive experience for me.

The speaker was a man by the name of Jason Sole, who was a motivational speaker. He embodied what it meant to truly reinvent yourself despite your circumstances. In true anxiety-ridden-me fashion, I spent the day of the event searching my thoughts for all that could go wrong and mentally talked myself out of going at least five times throughout that day.

I did, however, make it to the event and, as I walked down the hallway, I fought off my fight-or-flight mode, which generally made an appearance every time I was stepping outside my home. Walking inside the glass doors of the building, I had no idea my life was about to change forever.

That night, I walked into a room full of open-minded, forward-thinking individuals who allowed me to truly feel not just tolerated, but accepted, welcomed, and believed what I had to say actually mattered.

During the event, we all hung onto this enigma of a man's every word, a man who had somehow survived the Chicago and Minneapolis gang life and incarceration for several years. He reinvented himself despite it all—and within a system that was built to keep Black people oppressed.

Jason Sole is a Ph.D. scholar, author, university professor, social justice activist, and abolitionist. He's worked with legislators, police officers, prisons and even politicians to create real change and promote initiatives to dismantle systemic racism within Minnesota. Jason travels all over the country to provide the knowledge and tools other communities need to move in a positive direction in reimagining what social justice looks like within our Black and Brown communities.

A good friend and huge supporter of the work I've been

doing, Jason may never truly know what he really did for me that night he spoke in Alexandria back in 2019. Had I not been in that room and experienced that moment with so many like-minded community members who wanted to listen and learn—I would not have had the courage to reconnect with the Inclusion Network and developed the incredible friendships I forged in just a few short hours significantly impacted my lived experiences in Alexandria.

After Jason's presentation, he opened a Q&A session that became an open and frank conversation with me, Jason, and various members of the audience who all agreed that Alexandria needed a safe haven to have these difficult discussions without fear of retaliation.

In just a few short months, (with the support of the Inclusion Network), I was given an opportunity to create Voices Talk Show—a community, panel-based, talk series that explores hot button social issues in a safe space. The goal was to bring community members together to share stories, insight and educate one another on a variety of issues affecting our entire community.

In addition to the many hats piled on my head, by the summer of 2019, in just four short months of seeing Jason speak, I had added talk show host, producer and podcast host to my growing list of jobs!

I am never *not* shocked when I unveil yet another hidden piece of our history that has been taken from us as American people. So many buried truths that could have altered our present day completely. The American governing system has failed us in so many ways—most of which we may never truly know about. From the lost story of Fred Hampton to the Battle of Bamber Bridge (Homework! Look it up!)

Once in the second grade, we were learning about Christopher Columbus—you know, the same run of the mill—1492, Columbus sailed the ocean…Can you imagine the brain space we American-taught kids could free up in space that occupies that load of bullshit?! I mean—really! We're talking about new cures for our diseases, discovering the secret of immortality—the Fountain of Youth, if you will! But I digress.

I explicitly remember coming home and talking about this with my father. He was outraged at the outright lies that were printed in black and white in my history textbook. At the time, I didn't understand his anger and was mortified when he came to with me to school the next morning and in the most blunt and embarrassing way went off on my teacher about how he refuses to let his daughter recite lies about a man who murdered his way into our completely warped American history teachings. In true Virgo fashion, my dad, even whilst creating a scene outside of my classroom door, went on to school my teacher on the kind of man Christopher Columbus really was and how nearly destroyed the island we now call Haiti. Today, I can truly appreciate his crazy efforts to educate me in places American schooling failed to do so.

It never occurred to me that school could be the one place I couldn't count on to really learn about my unique history. Thus started my mission to know all the things the world has lost or have been deprived of. I learned more about my Haitian history as well, and it soon became a favorite topic for any major paper, report, or project I was assigned throughout my years in school. And every time, I learned something new I hadn't picked up on before.

RANDOM FACT: In 1803, about a year before the Haitian Revolution, Jean-Jacques Dessalines made a bold and powerful statement to his people when he created Haiti's flag. Using the French flag as a prototype, he ripped out the white strip in the center of the flag proclaiming he would rip the white colonizers out of Haiti. The remaining red and blue represented the Black Haitians and the red represented the Mulatto Haitians who made up most of the island's population at the time. At the center of the Haitian flag is Haiti's coat of arms.

Now an essential and powerful piece on the world board game, Haiti was the first independent Black nation on the planet in 1804, though we're the most neglected and forgotten of the African countries. They were the first and only ones to lead a successful slave rebellion—not one. Not two. But THREE times—defeating the French, Spanish, and the British. The Brits' ass whooping was so bad they've eliminated it from their nation's history altogether. (Source: Blashfield, Jean F. Haiti: Enchantment of the World. New York, NY: Scholastic Inc., 2008)

Our story as a people is more than revolutionary—it's the epitome of black excellence! In a world of only white powerhouses, our people rose up again and again, proving our rebel hearts could not and would not be eliminated. To be the first FREE Black nation at the peak of white supremacy is a tale they continue to sweep under the rug.

They don't want you to know how we changed the face of history. They don't want you to know the countless times we came to their nation's rescue only to be shown the service entrance in the back when they gathered to celebrate their "win." They don't want you to know there would've been no "American Revolution" without Haiti. Pay attention to who gets to write the history books. They likely left some details out.

I never set out to become a social justice warrior, but life had different plans for me. We plan and God laughs, right? Today, I am not just a content creator, I am also a racial justice speaker who often speaks at college events, diversity and equity events, community organizations and more. 2020 really helped me home in on my passion for justice and starting up important conversations about race, justice, equity and inclusion.

That summer of racial uprising inspired me to go even harder in my career endeavors. Lanau and I were both in a place where we felt the need to do our part. We participated in peaceful protests and supported and joined any effort that was bringing awareness to the realities of police brutality and the communities of color they were hunting and terrorizing.

In October of 2020, I partnered up with Jason and his organization, Humanize My Hoodie. Together, we were able to put together an event which was the very first social justice-based event I got to host on my own along with Jason. The event's purpose was to bring people within the community together within a safe space to discuss and hear a frank conversation.

We discussed police abolition and how we can create communities that are led with love, humanity, dignity and with REAL access to resources. It wasn't a giant bashing of police officers. It was an open discussion about reimagining what we see as justice. We talked about building communities that are focused on victims rather than criminals. We hypothesized what it would be to give people consequences over punishment and locking them up in a cell—further pushing people into delinquency, while chipping away their humanity.

I opened the event by telling my story in a way I never knew I'd have the courage to ever do out loud. But being in that room that day, amongst my brothers and sisters of color, allies from the community and beyond, empowered me in such a powerful way! My ancestors stood in that room with me that day, and I could feel them all around me. We had uncomfortable conversations, we shared our stories and Jason and I vibed on a whole other level.

I was proud of those in law enforcement who were brave enough to come with an open heart and listen. I know how difficult this was for many to take in but I'm glad I could be part of facilitating the conversation. I think what we all mostly took away was that our dreams for safer, more prosperous and inclusive communities were not that different. The event was a success, and I was hooked. For the first time I knew I was doing what I loved because it didn't feel like work at all.

At the start of 2021, I was granted the opportunity to work with Pioneer PBS in broadening what I produce on Voices Talk Show and expanding our reach beyond rural Minnesota. Broadcasting and TV hosting were never in the plans, but I find it to be the place I find myself most at ease.

My story is only just beginning, and I plan to continue to make a name and space for myself in the social justice world, as well as in television and/or radio. Just as I get to truly speak from the heart and be my authentic self on

Unapologetically Anxious Me—the podcast, I hope to one day have my own national platform in which I get to take part in important conversations that truly matter.

Jason Sole & I
Social Racial Justice
Speaking Event

Definitive Woman
Cover Girl
Summer 2018

Lanau Speaking Out
About Racism
Experiences
in Alexandria, MN

BLACK LIVES MATTER

"Say Their Names"
Protest
Summer 2020

Speaking at
"Time for Change"
Event
After George Floyd's
Murder

Filming
"Voices Talk Show"
Summer 2019

Chapter 14 ~ Unfinished Story

"I used to think I was the strangest person in the world but then I thought there are so many people in the world, there must be someone just like me who feels bizarre and flawed in the same ways I do. I would imagine her, and imagine that she must be out there thinking of me, too."

~Frida Kahlo

Being in and out of the hospital most of my life, I came to know my body and its inner workings better than most people before the age of 21. With my body having been through so much trauma, along with a general family history of fertility issues, I knew the path to motherhood for me would not be an easy one. For many years gynecologists would tell me how difficult it would be to have a child given my medical history.

Becoming a mother was something I had not just hoped for—I prayed for it. I spent many a night in my bed, literally pleading with God for it. The road to motherhood for me was the most heart-wrenching experience of my life. The older I got, the less I believed I was ever going to have a child of my own. At 19 going on 20, I got pregnant for the first time. I had no idea what was happening to me until I went to the doctor with bleeding—only to find out I was miscarrying at eight weeks.

Honestly, I didn't know how to feel because I really had a chance to process it or get attached. I shared the news with

Lanau who was sad for me but probably relieved given the fact that we were not really in a committed relationship, I was super young and he already had a baby with his ex.

Unfortunately, this was only one of four miscarriages I would experience before successfully delivering our first son together, Lenoxx, in the fall of 2013. I was 26 years old. Losing all those babies between 19 and 24 took a mental toll on me. I no longer felt like I was a real woman and with Lanau already being a father, the idea of not being able to have a child together with him made my heart ache.

One of our miscarriages was with twins and that one more than any other one hurt me to the core and to this day, I still can't help but wonder what would have happened had they survived. Lanau through all of it was always right there by my side, holding my hands and wiping my tears. Despite the miscarriages he was always positive we were going to have a family together even when I was ready to give up on the idea all together.

By the time we were ready to try again, almost as if it were fate, we conceived Lenoxx within just a few weeks of trying. Though it was a high-risk pregnancy given my history of miscarrying, I was put on bed rest from the very beginning and I did everything I could to deliver a healthy baby boy.

Lex's arrival changed me completely. Never did I know I held so much strength within me. Completely natural, I was able to deliver him after 10 hours of labor. Lanau and Carline were in the birth room with me, cheering me on and keeping me motivated. Unlike the movies, I didn't get to hold Lenoxx right away because he came out with the cord wrapped around his neck three times.

Immediately panicked the whole room turned into a scene from ER as a team of medical professionals with white coats stormed through the double doors. Their focus was our little boy who was only 5lbs and 11 ounces. Though Lanau remained by my side reassuring me everything was okay. I knew he was petrified and all we wanted to know was that our baby boy was fine.

Within a couple minutes—like letting the air slowly out of a balloon, the room breathed a collective sigh of relief as the doctor announced all was now well and that we could hold our little man. Having him in my arms with his tiny little finger clutching on to mine—I could not be happier. I was complete.

Three years later Katarina popped up on the scene and completely caught us off guard! The timing couldn't have been more wrong, and we weren't entirely sure we were doing the right thing by having the baby. We didn't find out we were pregnant until I was just about to enter my second trimester.

We'd just moved to Minnesota and were living with my sister-in-law, Michelle, along with our three nieces and nephew. We were not in a good place financially and having recently gone through so much with our families, the last thing we wanted, was to be shamed for being human.

Always the optimist, Lanau told me everything was going to be fine and that he knew this was the baby girl we'd always wanted. A couple weeks later we found out he was right after all and our baby girl was on the way.

Katarina's pregnancy was even harder and more high risk than Lenoxx's. I had extreme morning sickness that was all-day sickness and lasted the entire length of the pregnancy. I was losing weight rapidly because I was sick all the time and struggled to keep anything down. I felt extremely depressed being in a new place with no friends. By my fifth month, we were out of Michelle's place and living on our own.

I grew increasingly lonely and unhappy spending most days alone with just Lenoxx. Knowing how much I was struggling with my depression, Michelle checked in with me often and would still go with me to doctor's appointments. Lanau was working 10-to-12-hour days as the general manager of a local restaurant chain.

Our Katarina arrived in late April of 2016 and we were overjoyed to finally meet her. Michelle was a phlebotomist at the hospital at the time and just so happened to be the one who was called in to set up my vitals and put in my IV. I was lucky she decided to stay with me and Lanau during the birth which made us feel so much more at ease, having a familiar face we trusted. Eyes wide open, baby girl came out with a bang and completely stole our hearts.

Lex and Rina are the twin pillars on which I stand and the anchor to my life. If ever I did anything right in my life, it was them. They're my greatest success stories and by far the best accomplishment of my life. There's not a day that goes by that I am not absolutely grateful they chose me to be their mother.

More Beautiful Surprises

Lex was diagnosed with Autism Spectrum Disorder (ASD) in the spring of 2018. He was four years old, and after nearly six months of hopping from one facility to another, enduring a multitude of tests and evaluations, I was relieved to know that whatever was happening had nothing to do with me or my parenting.

We know our boy was always going to be a unique individual, whether he had ASD or not. Much like me, he has an almost innate connection to the written word and has been read to since his very first night on Earth. Never much of a joiner, he's always appreciated his space, and I've learned to just allow him to be the person he is meant to be.

By the time Lex was two, I knew something was different. His speech delay was my first indication. For a child who had consumed nearly two hundred books by the time he was one year old, Lex had absolutely no speech. For years we struggled to understand him and worked almost obsessively with him to give him any form of communication to make his life, and ours, a lot calmer.

My next and probably most obvious sign of Lex's ASD was his increasingly intense behavior. Everything felt like a battle, and it became a nightmare to accomplish even the simplest of tasks, like going to the grocery store or cooking dinner for my family. Nearly every day ended with my sobbing into a pillow, feeling like I had somehow, someway failed him.

As nutty as it may sound, Lenoxx's ASD diagnosis was a relief to hear. The minute the therapist said it, it all made sense. I hadn't failed my child. There was a medical and scientific reason behind all of our struggles—and suddenly, I could breathe.

Of course, I'm human, and that small moment of relief quickly turned to panic as I began thinking about what autism even meant. I had a basic idea of what it was (or so

I thought, at the time). I had just never thought about it in relation to my own child. From what I gathered from the media and TV shows, an autistic person was unemotional and withdrawn, none of which seemed to apply to our Lenoxx.

I wasn't worried about how well Lex was going to do in the outside world. I worry about what the outside world will do to him. My perspective was instantly altered when an amazing woman in my life told me to stop, breathe and ask myself, "What has changed?" The reality was that Lenoxx was—still my Lenoxx. The only thing that had changed was me.

Before Katarina was two, we began recognizing some of the same signs in her as we'd observed in Lenoxx at the same age. Though her early years were complicated and rough due to an infected ear pit she was born with, her autism showed up in different ways than Lex's did as well. While Lex began taking his first steps around his 9th month, Rina in contrast didn't take her first step until she was 19 months old. Until then she scooched everywhere like a cute, non-creepy Smeagol that made Lanau and I crack up. She was just so damn cute!

Over the few years, Lanau and I have consumed every piece of literature and media surrounding autism. I talked to friends and family about everything I was learning and rallied with my community of therapists, paraprofessionals, personal care assistants (PCAs), doctors, and teachers to give Lex and Rina everything they needed to be successful.

Lenoxx is now seven years old and Katarina is soon to be five years old. They're both super chatty with Rina learning to talk up a storm more and more every day, whether you're listening to her or not. I absolutely LOVE it! Both Lex and

Rina's behaviors have calmed down, and I can see how confident they both are in all that they take on. Lex is in kindergarten and Rina is heading into another round of preschool in the same program Lenoxx was in before he started kindergarten.

Though Lex will probably always choose a good book over a party any day and Rina may never give up the concept of being a "but-ter-ply pin-cess," I can't wait to see what their absolutely brilliant minds will do as they grow from children into adulthood. Despite being on the spectrum, our babies are the most loving and gentle-hearted little people we know! They may not always be able to verbalize it eloquently, but they show it in spades all the time.

In our home, we do stimming—a lot. We love our routines. We repeat ourselves constantly. We meltdown and actively practice having calm bodies and gentle hands. We love lining things up. We watch the same things over and over again. In our home, we believe and we pray hard—we love even harder. Autism is living with us. We are not living with autism.

I love my parents more than they'll ever truly know but when it came down to it, I had to choose "me" because the family I'd created needed me. Just me. After the summer of 2015, my relationship with my parents was forever altered when they gave me the ultimatum I'd feared had been brewing for years: choosing between them and my husband.

Though painful, it was an easy decision to make, and I didn't even hesitate. Unfortunately, culture, perspective, and life experiences may never bring my parents and me to a place of understanding. Little by little, I'm working on "radically accepting" that, as my hired friend would say. Still, every now and then, my heart breaks a little when I think of how much both sets of their grandparents are missing and how much our kids deserve grandparents who are active in their lives, or at the very least, want to see them blossom and grow.

My grandmother's presence though limited, rare and scarce in my life growing up, she influenced the person I am today, and I feel I would've been lost without her random spouts of wisdom. I always wanted my kids to have the same but much more present.

My parents at least had the excuse of our grandparents being in a completely different country being the only barrier that kept them from being in our lives regularly. But my parents live right here in the states with me. Very far apart but still only a flight away if they truly desired to do so. It's a part of my family and culture I still toil to understand even today.

If I could openly and freely say one thing to my parents right now and not just have them listen but truly hear me, I'd want them to know:

I married the man you always wanted for me, and I am the mother you raised me to be. My husband is kind, gentle and the most hardworking human being I've ever met. My children have a mother and father who will move heaven and Earth to give them a childhood they don't have to recover from. Most importantly, I want you to know I am happy and will always love you both—even if it's from a distance. THIS was my American Dream. Your sacrifices were not made in vain.

People used to always ask me if I felt I had missed out on life by getting married so young and only having experienced one man. But I never have. Growing up the way I did, I consider myself to be immensely favored by God to have been blessed with a man like Lanau. Through our ups and downs, we only held on tighter to our love. As cheesy as it may be, Lanau is my soulmate and my one true love.

I know this because he rescued me from a life of abuse at the hands of what could've been awful men, had I not been led to him.

Nearly 17 years together and approaching the ninth year of our marriage, I fall more and more in love with my husband every day. There aren't many moments in the day that aren't flooded with thoughts of him and I am blessed that he also feels the same way. Now, with our perfect little family of four, we have created the kind of love that most people could only dream of—it's that evergreen kind of love.

~FOR LOVE ALONE~

About the Author

Josette "Jo" Ciceron is a born writer. She has spent most of her life navigating the art of the written word. As a college student at University of South Florida in Tampa, she discovered her love for journalism and storytelling. Never giving up on her true love—writing—at 33-years-old she continues to write, even if it is not in a professional capacity.

Today Jo is the proud momma of her life's anchors, Lenoxx and Katarina, whom she and her hubby lovingly refer to as Lex & Rina. A hopeless romantic, she takes pride in being a wife to her life partner, soulmate, and greatest love—Lanau—who has played a major role in her development as a creator, woman, mother, and even as an activist.

In the summer of 2018, Jo's life's trajectory took a major turn when she went public with her stories of racism and discrimination in small, predominantly white, Alexandria, Minnesota. A lifelong fan of the series Gilmore Girls, she believed she was moving to Minnesota's version of Stars Hollow. She very quickly learned that the pleasantries of small-town life only existed in movies and TV shows.

In a unique mix of Haitian and American culture, and the unpredictable life of a Black girl-turned-woman, Jo has embraced her vulnerabilities and imperfections. Follow along as she learns the best lessons life has to teach her as she bravely unveils her little corner of the world.

Starting out as a freelance writer for several years after college, she has been the Associate Editor of a woman's publication, *Definitive Woman Magazine*, based-in Alexandria, MN since Jo has stretched her content creation talents beyond writing by hosting the impactful YouTube series, Voices Talk Show—an entity of the Inclusion Network of Alexandria, MN. Jo was instrumental in developing the show's concept and creating the series in the Fall of 2019. The show has earned a partnership with Pioneer PBS, which Jo will be producing and hosting as well. Learn more about Jo Ciceron from her podcast Unapologetically Anxious Me: Confessions of a Haitian Girl in Small-Town Minnesota, through Apple Podcasts, Stitcher and Spotify.

Special Thanks

Because of you my dream turned into reality…
~Thank you.

- ❖ Jason Sole
- ❖ Heather Hauptli
- ❖ Deb LeDoux
- ❖ Lauren Larson
- ❖ Nicole Mulder
- ❖ James Pence
- ❖ Preeti Yonjon Feist
- ❖ Mattison Bogart
- ❖ Tracy Bogart
- ❖ Tessie Rangel
- ❖ Amy Swart
- ❖ Sylvia Luetmer
- ❖ Scott Keehn
- ❖ Bonnie Fulghum
- ❖ Sophie Burnevik
- ❖ Kristina Sherrett
- ❖ Molly Larbre
- ❖ Carolyn Philstrom
- ❖ Amanda Hart
- ❖ Kimberly Cronk
- ❖ Aaron Sands
- ❖ Rosanna Seabold
- ❖ Katherine Harrison
- ❖ Josie Zimmerman
- ❖ Miranda Posthumus
- ❖ Elizabeth Hossfeld

- ❖ Meegan Hall
- ❖ Jamie Andycha
- ❖ Valerie Hall
- ❖ Katy Kruse
- ❖ Janelle Koscinski
- ❖ Rebecca Byrne
- ❖ Jenn James
- ❖ Julie Zueleke

Organizations

- ❖ Inclusion Network of Alexandria
- ❖ Humanize My Hoodie
- ❖ Theatre L'Homme Dieu

Design

- ❖ Jennifer Guenther (cover photography)
- ❖ Kerry Browen (cover design)

Made in the USA
Columbia, SC
06 September 2021